TAKE
THE
NIGHT
CHALLENGE

DR. GREG & ERIN SMALLEY

TAKE
THE

d❤️te

NIGHT
CHALLENGE

52 Creative Ideas to
Make Your Marriage Fun

Colorado Springs, Colorado

Take the Date Night Challenge
Copyright © 2013 Focus on the Family

ISBN: 978-1-58997-770-9

Focus on the Family and the accompanying logo and design are federally registered trademarks of Focus on the Family, Colorado Springs, CO 80995. Date Night Challenge is a trademark of Focus on the Family.

All Scripture quotations, unless otherwise indicated, are taken from the *Holy Bible, New International Version*®. NIV®. Copyright © 1973, 1978, 1984 by Biblica, Inc.™ Used by permission of Zondervan. All rights reserved worldwide (www.zondervan.com). Scripture quotations marked NASB are taken from the *New American Standard Bible*®, Copyright © 1960, 1962, 1963, 1968, 1971, 1972, 1973, 1975, 1977, 1995 by The Lockman Foundation. Used by permission. (www.Lockman.org.)

Italicized words in Bible verses were added by the authors for emphasis.

The use of material from or references to various websites does not imply endorsement of those sites in their entirety. Availability of websites and pages is subject to change without notice.

No part of this publication may be reproduced, stored in a retrieval system, or transmitted in any form or by any means—electronic, mechanical, photocopy, recording, or otherwise—without prior written permission of Focus on the Family.

Editorial contributors: Don Morgan, Megan Gordon, and Marianne Hering
Cover design by the CSK Group

Library of Congress Cataloging-in-Publication Data is available for this book by contacting the Library of Congress at http://www.loc.gov/help/contact-general.html.

Printed in the United States of America
1 2 3 4 5 6 7 8 9 /19 18 17 16 15 14 13

To Gary and Norma Smalley and Pat and Rosalie Murphy—as our parents, thank you for modeling lifelong marriages full of love and laughter.

To our good friends Tim and Beth Popadic— your passion for helping couples unleash the power of a regular date night inspires us!

Contents

Why Date after You're Married?

Picture this scene: A young man is driving through city streets. He has cleaned out his car for the first time in months. He dressed to look as much like Ryan Gosling as possible and worries that maybe he should have shaved off his goatee. At a stoplight, he keys in a text and sends it to the girl he'll be meeting in less than ten minutes. He heads toward his destination with a sense of excitement and anticipation—and more than a little nervousness.

Across town, a young woman's cell phone beeps. She reads the text and feels the lump in her stomach tighten. *Just ten more minutes.* She's happy but oh so anxious. She shoves three lip gloss tubes into her purse; she's not sure which color is best. She checks her reflection in the mirror to make sure her jeans look good. As she arranges her bangs for what seems like the thousandth time, her nervousness is tempered by an overriding sense of enthusiasm.

Can you feel the electricity in the air? Obviously, these two love-struck people are getting ready to go on a date. They're looking forward to spending time with each other. They have both invested thought and effort in preparing themselves for the occasion, and they're relishing the opportunity to enjoy one another's company. The man and woman both understand that going on a date will help them get to know each other better and develop a deeper bond. And while forging a relationship is serious business, especially when that relationship may be headed toward marriage, they also understand that dating, at its core, is *fun*.

Can you remember what that felt like? Do you recall the rush of adrenaline you experienced at the thought of spending a fun evening with a certain attractive someone? Obviously, you and your spouse dated prior to getting married, and you almost certainly enjoyed it. Even if you came from an environment in which dating was frowned upon and courtship was considered the only appropriate precursor to matrimony, there were likely occasions when your relationship deepened and flourished through good conversation over a fun, shared activity.

Think about some of those good times you and your spouse spent together prior to tying the knot. Can you remember the excitement? The sense of discovery? Can you recall what it felt like to learn about his or her favorite childhood memories? To talk about the experiences—both good and bad—that made each of you who you were at the time? To spend time laughing, talking, praying, and sharing your dreams, only to realize, at the end of the process, that you had fallen in love? What a magnificent experience!

"Yes, but that was then and this is now," you might be saying. "We're married! We don't need to pursue each other anymore. It's a done deal. We learned all we needed to learn about each other during the seasons of dating and engagement, and now it's full steam ahead. We're one flesh, baby! And besides, who has time to go gallivanting around town like a couple of college kids? There are more than a few other things competing for our attention at the moment, not the least of which is raising our kids to respect God, and pursuing gainful employment, and . . ."

Most likely, your relationship has changed dramatically since the days before you were married. But that change has probably been gradual. Maybe even after you said "I do," you enjoyed a few years of postnuptial dating. In a certain sense, those years prior to having kids were especially exciting. Before marriage, you had to have certain physical and spiritual barriers in place to guard against going too far sexually. But after marriage, those restrictions disappeared, and you could experience physical intimacy at the end of your date with God's blessing.

Eventually, though, all of that wonderful sex resulted in *pregnancy*. That's a good thing! It's the beauty of God's design for physical intimacy between husband and wife. But it can definitely bring challenges and changes to a relationship that, up until that point, had been defined as "just the two of us." You know what we mean. You've cleaned throw-up from every imaginable surface in the house and the car. You've made frantic trips to the emergency room in the middle of the night with a feverish child. You've had plenty of shouting matches with your teen after she missed her curfew *again*. As for romance, the last time you tried to invoke the aura of Song of Solomon in the bedroom, you were interrupted by an unmistakable *tap, tap, tap* on the bedroom door: "Mommy, Daddy, are you in there?" And just as things were getting interesting!

And again, you might be saying, "That's okay, Greg and Erin. Really. It's all good. We signed up for this parenting thing, and we don't expect to be able to return to those romantic days of youthful love. We're now in a different season of life, and someday we'll pick up where we left off and be 'married' again."

Unfortunately, that mind-set rarely leads to a happy marriage.

And if we're honest, in God's design for marriage, couples aren't supposed to take a break from emotional intimacy. You may add new titles to your lives as the years go by—"parent," "manager," "homemaker," and so on. But through it all, you still retain the titles you were given by the pastor when you were first married: husband and wife! You have added additional titles and roles as the years have passed, but you still are, and always will remain, husband and wife.

Perhaps you've had two or three kids by now. You love them more than life itself. You wouldn't trade them for anything. And yet sometimes, you look back on your years of dating, both prior to and after marriage, and you wonder what happened. You miss having "couple time"—the opportunity to relax, connect, and just focus on each other without distraction.

But even as you fondly reminisce about those years of dating, your resistance starts to increase. "C'mon, Greg and Erin!" you might be saying. "Please don't lay a guilt trip on us. We have more than we can handle in our lives as it is. The kids have school and all kinds of extracurricular activities. My job involves at least a week of travel per month. My parents are getting older and require extra care. I'm serving on four different committees between school and church. We're so tired we can barely see straight, and you're asking us to add a date night to our endless list of responsibilities? Get real!"

Believe us, we know how you feel! Our lives are chaotic too. Such is the nature of life in the twenty-first century, for better or worse. We've been married since 1992, and in the years since that time, we've added new challenges and responsibilities to our lives on what seems like a daily basis. We have four kids who, as of this writing, range from preschool age to college age, and there hasn't been a day in raising them when we've said, "Hey, this is supereasy!" And it isn't just the kids who are a challenge. We've traveled across the country and around the world leading marriage seminars for pastors, professionals, and lay leaders. Greg has pursued a doctorate in psychology as well as a counseling degree, has worked for the Center for Relationship Enrichment at John Brown University, has served as president of the National Institute of Marriage, has written eleven books, and currently serves as executive director of Marriage and Family Formation at Focus on the Family.

This is not to brag. It's only to say that it's hard—*incredibly* hard, sometimes—for us to make the time necessary to invest in our husband-wife relationship, with no distractions. The professional and ministerial work of studying marriage and helping others build stronger marriages doesn't leave us much room to invest quality time in our own! And yet we make it happen.

In our counseling experiences, we've seen too many couples who try to coast through the childrearing and career years without making time to deepen and nurture their own marriages. It's a recipe for disaster.

Those couples who don't date may achieve financial stability, and they might even successfully raise their kids and navigate them through school. But they reach the empty-nest years and realize that they're strangers living under the same roof. By then, it's incredibly difficult to reverse the damage wrought by decades of essentially ignoring each other and clinging to the false assumption that they can pick up at fifty-five exactly where they left off at twenty-five.

The Case for Date Night

We're not suggesting that simply cramming a date night into your already overcrowded schedule is going to prevent you from experiencing the unfortunate scenario we just described. But a commitment to date nights done right can definitely play a significant part in an overall plan to be *intentional* about investing in the health of your marriage.

"But how?" you might be asking. "We don't have time, and besides, we're fine."

We'll get to the "how" in the next chapters. But first let's explore some common-sense reasons why committing to a *regular* date night can revolutionize your marriage:

1. *Date nights are critical for the health of your relationship.* Marriage relationships are dynamic; they are alive and always changing. And just like any relationship, marriages need to be fed and stimulated to stay alive and grow.

2. *Date nights help you get reacquainted.* The notion that you already know all there is to know about your spouse is a myth. There's *always* something new to learn about your spouse, because we all change. Dating is a great way to update and deepen your knowledge of your beloved. It's vital that you keep that curiosity and interest in your mate flourishing.

3. *Date nights are a great investment in the future.* Just like a savings account, the more you invest in your relationship, the more it will grow exponentially over time. Dates also lay the framework for future times together, encouraging you and your spouse to look forward to spending more time together.

4. *Date nights put the focus back on your marriage.* As you well know, day-to-day distractions pull your attention away from your spouse. Dates help you refocus and put that person back at the top of your priority list. When a date night is going the way it should, the only thing the two of you have to concentrate on is each other. (More on this later!)

5. *Date nights help you remember the good times.* A good date will often bring up fond premarriage memories. Recalling these memories can help you and your spouse generate positive feelings and anticipation for your next date.

6. *Date nights send a positive message.* To your friends, family, and especially your kids, marriage needs to be viewed as something valuable and precious. Marriage is something important enough to put ongoing effort into. And date nights communicate to your spouse that he or she is valuable enough to you that you won't give all of your prime time to other people or things.

7. *Date nights strengthen the marital bond.* The more time you and your spouse spend alone enjoying each other, the stronger your bond becomes. This naturally deepens your intimacy and brings you closer together.

8. *Date nights are a great way to reconnect.* Dating helps you unplug from your busy and hectic pace of life to simply enjoy being together.

9. *Date nights rekindle the romance in your relationship.* Having a night out with your spouse is an important part of keeping romance alive.

10. *Date nights inject excitement into a stale marriage.* Under the stress of work, household duties, and childrearing, spouses can become nothing more than distant roommates. Just like the young couple at the beginning of this chapter, spouses need to feel that rush of excitement and adrenaline from time to time. They must never succumb to the idea that their marriage is simply a recycled union of two tired and bored souls.

11. *Date nights help you both decompress.* Every couple needs a chance to enjoy each other's company without being weighed down by the demands of life. A date night should be free from the distractions of children, extended family, friends, or work. It should represent an opportunity for you to rediscover the person you fell in love with. We'll explore this concept in much greater detail in the next chapter.

12. *Date nights strengthen your commitment.* By making date night a priority, you are communicating to your spouse that divorce is out of the question and that you're committed to strengthening your marriage by spending ongoing quality time together.

Granted, you don't really need us to tell you that spending uninterrupted quality time together is good for your marriage. But did you know there's a growing body of scientific research that illuminates and confirms these same concepts about the importance of marital dating?

Take, for example, the prestigiously named Survey of Marital Generosity (SMG), a national study of more than sixteen hundred married couples ages eighteen to fifty-five that was conducted in 2010 and 2011 by the National Marriage Project at the University of Virginia. This detailed survey cited a wealth of additional social-science data confirming that couples who had date nights experienced enhanced communication, a greater sense of marital excitement and novelty, increased emphasis on romantic love and sexuality, a deeper sense of commitment, and a decrease in stress.[1] In other words, many of the common-sense benefits of marital date nights we just outlined are confirmed by a wealth of scientific data.

Even more specifically, the Survey of Marital Generosity found a strong connection between "one-on-one couple time and relationship quality,"[2] which is a broader category that could include not only structured date nights but also other alone time between married couples. For example, the SMG found that "husbands and wives who engaged in couple time with their mates at least once a week were approximately 3.5 times *more likely* to report being 'very happy' in their marriages," compared to those who spent less quality time together.[3] Couples who spent weekly couple time together also reported dramatically higher rates of satisfaction in their communication and sexual satisfaction (both to the tune of a 300 percent increase!), and in their levels of commitment to each other (a 250 percent increase).[4] The authors of the study concluded that "couples who devote time specifically to one another at least once a week are markedly more likely to enjoy high-quality relationships and lower divorce rates, compared to couples who do not devote much couple time to one another."[5]

Finally, our own research testifies to the validity of these studies. Greg spearheaded a date-night program a few years ago when he was working with Northwest Arkansas Healthy Marriages. Soon after, our good friend Tim Popadic orchestrated Date Night Challenge events in West Palm Beach, Florida, in 2011 and 2012. We surveyed the couples who participated in the Florida Date Night Challenges and discovered that a whopping 92 percent of them saw an increase in their relationship satisfaction. That's an astonishingly good rate of return!

Since Greg came to Focus on the Family to assume the role of executive director of Marriage and Family Formation, we've seen the date-night concept explode. Focus now hosts an annual Date Night Challenge, a live event that is produced as a DVD to be used by churches, Bible studies, and small groups worldwide. Our 2012 Date Night Challenge saw participation from more than nine hundred churches, representing all fifty states as well as several countries around the world.

The concept itself is simple: We challenge couples to go on three dates in three weeks and then commit to one date per month for a year. And without fail, we hear from husbands and wives whose relationships are invigorated, reenergized, and revitalized as a result of participating in the Date Night Challenge. We're convinced that after reading this book and making a similar commitment to date your mate on a regular basis, you will share their enthusiasm.

"This is all well and good," you may say. "But it's easier said than done."

You're right! It might not be easy, but it *is* possible. In the next chapter we'll outline some simple strategies you can employ to not only make date nights *possible* in your marriage but to also make them the rewarding, fulfilling, *fun* occasions they're supposed to be. Onward and upward!

Dating That's Fun and Not a Chore to Be Done!

Remember the couple at the beginning of chapter 1? You know—the guy who's driving confidently across town and the girl who's anxiously preparing for the moment he arrives on her doorstep. They're eager to spend time together. They're in love. They're getting ready to go on a *date*!

But now, think about how differently the scene might turn out if one or both of them viewed their imminent date as a chore or an obligation. Imagine the young man arriving at the girl's door, and instead of complimenting her on her dress, he says something along the lines of, "Okay, I'm here. But I have a lot going on in my life right now, and I don't really have much time for the dating scene. Let's get this over with!"

Or maybe it's the girl who is less than enthusiastic. She answers the door and says, "Well, the books I've read suggest that dating is necessary for us to get to know each other better and determine whether we might be compatible in marriage. I suppose going on a few dates with you is something I'm obliged to do as your girlfriend and potential life partner. Let's go!"

Uh-oh. Did you hear all the air go out of the balloon? What a terrible way to start a date! We can almost guarantee that if, during your single years, you kicked off a date with a "Let's get this over with" attitude, it was probably your final date with that person. No one wants to spend time with someone who's treating that time as something that's obligatory or compulsory.

And yet, that's *exactly* the way many married couples view dating, if they even consider it at all. The spark is gone. The thrill is gone. They're distracted by kids and jobs and responsibilities, and maybe deep down they feel it may be somehow sinful or inappropriate for them to actually inject some *fun* into their married life. But they don't want to end up in divorce court, so they submit themselves to an occasional date night in an effort to create the illusion that they're still emotionally connected. Date night, when it happens, is a chore, an obligation, another appointment to cram into an already maxed-out calendar. Like grocery shopping or going to the dentist, it's something they feel they're *supposed* to do, not something they *want* to do.

If this is your perspective on marital dating—if this is your attitude reading this book—then throw that negative thinking out the window right now! Dating *can* and *should* be fun, right now, at this busy stage of your married life. It isn't a chore. It isn't an obligation. Consider these wise words from Dolores Curran in her excellent book *Traits of a Healthy Family*:

> The primary hallmark of a strong family seems to be its absence of guilt at times of play. Individuals and the family collectively give themselves permission to sit back, relax, dream, and enjoy. Further, they schedule play times onto the calendar; they don't wait for free time.[1]

True, it might require more effort to make date night happen than it did in those carefree days prior to marriage, but dating for fun is possible. You just need to be intentional about it. You just need to have a strategy. Think of some of the other fun things you do as a family, whether going on vacation, heading to the mountains for a camping trip, or even just going to the movies or out for dinner. Each of those things, to one degree or another, requires planning and intentionality. They don't just happen unless you're willing to do what it takes to make them happen. So it is with marital dating.

Obviously, putting the fun in dating begins with an attitude of the heart. You might go on a date to the biggest and best amusement park in the country, but if your heart isn't in it, you're not going to have a good time. Amusement parks are designed for people who *want* to be there, not for those who have to be dragged through the front gate kicking and screaming. On the other hand, the very simplest of dates, even just taking a casual walk hand in hand around the park, can be incredibly enjoyable if you and your spouse have your hearts in the right place—if you *want* to be there and you *want* to enjoy each other's company and you *want* to invest in your relationship and you *want* to foster deeper intimacy. Are you seeing a theme here? You gotta want it!

Of course, having your heart in the right place isn't something that applies only to date night. It's part of a larger strategy in marriage that involves expressing interest, attention, and curiosity toward your spouse. Marriage researcher Dr. John Gottman describes this process of relating and connecting as "turning toward" your spouse.[2] Couples who "turn toward" each other literally shift their focus from work, kids, and other distractions of the day to focus their attention on their spouse. It could be something as simple as complimenting your wife on her appearance as you prepare to leave for church or making sure to give each other a kiss good-bye before you go your separate ways in the morning. Even in brief exchanges like these, husband and wife are choosing to turn *toward* each other instead of away.

Dr. Gottman has studied hundreds of married couples, and his research testifies to the power of turning toward your spouse on a consistent basis. His studies show that loving, romantic relationships typically thrive not as a result of lavish vacations or extravagant gifts but through small everyday acts. Happy, thriving couples take time to talk to each other, to laugh from time to time, and to pay close attention to what the other is doing or saying. Every day, in small ways, they *turn toward* one another instead of ignoring or turning away from each other. Gottman says, "Couples who turn toward each other remain emotionally engaged and stay married. . . . Turning toward is the basis of emotional connection, romance, passion, and a good sex life."[3]

No matter how busy you may be, and Lord knows all of us are busy, you should never be too busy to turn toward your spouse on a daily basis. Consider this powerful statement from Barack Obama when he was asked by *Ebony* magazine in 2007 how he was able to keep his marriage healthy in the midst of a busy political career:

> What I realize as I get older is that Michelle is less concerned about me giving her flowers than she is that I'm doing things that are hard for me—carving out time. That to her is proof, evidence that I'm thinking about her. She appreciates the flowers, but to her romance is that I'm actually paying attention to

things that she cares about, and time is always an important factor.[4]

Did you catch that? Love him or hate him, Mr. Obama appears to have a firm grasp of the concept of turning toward his spouse. And although he made that statement prior to becoming president of the United States, we'd like to think he's still doing what he can to maintain that commitment to his wife.

So what's your excuse? We know you're busy. But if the president can turn toward his wife amid the distractions of politics, fiscal "cliffs," and having control of a vast nuclear arsenal, so can you. And date nights are a critical part of that equation.

With that said, let's look at a few practical ways to make sure your dates are the most *fun, exciting, intimacy-building* events they can be. We've learned, both from our own experiences and from our counseling work with other couples, a few of the dos and one significant don't associated with marital dating. Put the following principles into practice, and you'll be well on the road to a fun dating experience that you'll want to repeat again and again.

Don't: Administrate Your Marriage

Okay, let's get the big "don't" out of the way right off the bat. One of the first mistakes that married couples make when they head out on a date is that they use the time not to have fun and enjoy each other's company but to tackle all of the problems they may be facing. This is understandable to a certain extent. We've already established the fact that for most couples, time is extremely limited. It's hard enough to carve out a few hours for a date once a month, so why not use that time to get some stuff done? Some couples may even try to put a "holy spin" on this idea, believing that it's inappropriate for them to go out and simply have fun. They feel they should be "making the most of every opportunity, because the days are evil" (Ephesians 5:16).

And so, when it's time for a date, they have a long list of issues that need to be handled. Grievances that need to be addressed. Contentious problems that need to be brought out into the light. And before you know it, what started out as a fun date (at least in theory) becomes another harsh dose of reality in an already exhausting week. At the end of the date, husband and wife feel even more frustrated, tense, and disillusioned than when they began. There's no emotional connection. No shared intimacy.

Believe us, we aren't immune to this problem. There have been times when we've planned a date night, carved out a few hours on the calendar, paid a babysitter . . . and then proceeded to spend the evening arguing about a contentious or stressful issue on the home front. Whenever this happens, one of us usually asks, "Why did we just pay a babysitter for the privilege of going out and arguing? We can argue at home!"

Case in point: early in our marriage, we decided to spend a day at Disneyland, just the two of us. (*Note:* Don't worry; not every date needs to be a big "event" like this!) Before entering the park, we stopped at a nearby sandwich shop for lunch. As we sat eating, I (Greg) decided to bring up a rather sensitive issue in our marriage. The discussion became rather heated, and voices were raised to the point that we decided to continue the discussion in the parking lot rather than embarrass ourselves (and others) in the restaurant.

Unfortunately, moving the discussion outside didn't help. The argument continued, and with no resolution in sight, we decided to go home. It just didn't seem right to spend a day at "the happiest place on earth" while we were fuming at each other. It ended up taking the rest of the day at home to resolve the issue, but by then, the damage was done. We had missed a wonderful opportunity to have fun together, build memories, and enjoy each other's company. Why? Because we had succumbed to the temptation to "administrate" our marriage during our date.

Here's an important point of clarification, though: Date nights are not about avoidance. Every marriage has real issues that need to be addressed on a regular basis. From discipline issues with kids to financial challenges, career decisions, communication struggles, and genuine hurts between spouses, there's a time and place to confront the challenges facing your marriage. If you're pursuing mindless fun on your dates as a means of avoiding talking about the serious issues, you're only going to do further harm. Time and energy *must* be set aside to deal with your marriage and family "issues."

But again, date nights aren't the time for this important activity. Your dates need to be fun, exciting, and *conflict-free*. There are valid and, yes, even scientific reasons for this, as we'll discover a little later in this chapter. When you head out on your next date, perhaps your theme verse shouldn't be "making the most of every opportunity, because the days are evil," but something more along the lines of "May you rejoice in the wife of your youth" (Proverbs 5:18).

Do: Stay Current

Many young people get married and believe they can have their spouse totally figured out after the first year or so. Actually, some may even believe that they can have their future mate completely pegged *before* tying the knot. In some ways, our Christian subculture may contribute to this misconception. We tell engaged couples to make sure they really and truly *know* each other—their likes and dislikes, their character traits, their quirks and idiosyncrasies—prior to making the ultimate commitment of marriage. We encourage them to engage in premarital counseling to dig even deeper into their values and spiritual beliefs. Some people complete this process and think, *Wow, that was intense! I'm so glad I have my betrothed figured out now so that I can proceed into this marriage with eyes wide open.*

Now don't get us wrong. Premarital counseling is very important when it comes to getting to know your future mate. The first year of marriage is also a critical time of learning and growing together. But let's face it; people are always changing. Throughout your life, as you grow and mature, you evolve emotionally and spiritually. Your opinion on certain issues may vary over time. Your faith will go through times of testing and refining. Most people would agree that they aren't the same person at age fifty that they were at age twenty.

Most married couples know this, and they assume they'll perceive these changes in their spouse by simple virtue of the fact that they're both living under the same roof. But it's amazing how things can slip past your radar when you're occupied with raising kids, pursuing your career, volunteering at church, keeping up with the bills, fixing up the house, and so on. Sometimes there may be things going on in your spouse's life of which you're totally unaware. We're not talking about sinful, secretive things that your spouse may be trying to hide; we're talking about general changes in his or her tastes, preferences, and beliefs that can slip past you simply because you're not paying attention.

For example, a few years ago Erin called me (Greg) at work and asked me to pick up a few items at the grocery store on my way home. Later that evening, I stopped at the store, procured the items, and then, on my way to the checkout lane, noticed a massive display of Diet Coke. My eyes lit up immediately because I knew it was Erin's very favorite beverage. She drank it at every opportunity. She might have it at lunch or dinner or as an afternoon pick-me-up. It was like the nectar of life for her! She didn't go so far as to pour it over her breakfast cereal in the morning, but even that didn't seem outside the realm of possibility.

In any event, I added a case of Diet Coke to my cart. In my mind, it was the most thoughtful gesture imaginable. I knew Erin would swoon with love when she saw me come through the door with such a heartfelt surprise for her!

The outcome wasn't quite what I envisioned, however. When I presented Erin with the Diet Coke, she looked at me sympathetically and said, "Awww . . . I don't drink that anymore!"

I was shocked! The fact of the matter was that Erin hadn't drunk Diet Coke for some time. She had given it up in favor of water and other more healthy beverages. But I just hadn't noticed. I took for granted the fact that Erin was the same Diet Coke–lovin' woman I had married, when in reality she had long since moved on.

What does all this have to do with marital dating? Two things. First of all, as you plan your dates, make sure you're paying attention to your spouse and his or her *current* likes and dislikes. He may have been a big Frisbee golf fan when you first got married, but is that still the case? She may have enjoyed going out for milkshakes when you were dating, but is that what she wants now after two kids and an earnest desire to watch her weight? Be sensitive to what your spouse is thinking and feeling *now* as you consider your date-night activities.

A second reason why staying current is important to marital dating is because dates are a perfect opportunity for you and your spouse to play catch-up with each other! As you think about planning your date, you may be panicking because you realize that you've fallen victim to the very problem we outlined earlier: You've been so busy with real life that you really don't know what your spouse's likes and dislikes are anymore. Don't sweat it! Going on regular dates is an excellent opportunity for you and your spouse to get reacquainted, so to speak, and to learn new things about one another. When you were dating prior to marriage, you were no doubt incessantly curious about your potential mate and asked question after question. Adopt that approach again! No matter how much you think you know about your spouse, there's always something new to learn.

Do: Try New and Exciting Activities

Okay, now let's return, for the third time, to the young couple we first met at the beginning of the book. We established at the time that they're both *excited* about their imminent date. Why? Because the entire experience is new for them. They're still in the process of getting to know each other. From dinner to movies to sporting events to hiking to double dates with friends to church gatherings, they're thrilled with the chance to experience new things within the context of their budding relationship.

But there's something much deeper going on here than just an affectionate young couple doing entertaining things together. There are actually physiological changes taking place in their brains—changes that contribute significantly to the process of what we might call "falling in love." As the young man and woman look forward to their time together, and especially as they experience new activities together during the course of their dates, their brains release dopamine and norepinephrine, neurotransmitters that help control the brain's reward and pleasure centers. Obviously, there's a lot more to falling in love than just these chemicals. But a significant degree of the excitement and anticipation that young couples in love feel—the rush and the feeling of "butterflies" in the stomach—can be attributed to the release of these neurotransmitters in the brain.

Now, you may remember what this felt like when you and your future spouse went out on your first few dates. It was a great feeling, wasn't it? It was exciting to be young and in love. But after you got married, familiarity set in, and you no longer got the same rush that you felt as a young Romeo and Juliet. It's not that you don't love each other anymore; it's just that you don't experience that same feeling of exhilaration when you spend time together.

However, the fact of the matter is that if you endeavor to inject your marital dates with the elements of *novelty* and *fun*, your brains will, in fact, trigger the same dopamine and norepinephrine that made you feel so giddy and euphoric when your love first began to bloom!

Again, the keys are *novelty* and *fun*. Simply spending quality time together isn't enough. It's a good start, of course, but to make that time even more enjoyable and to trigger those neurotransmitters, you're going to have to mix things up a bit. Going to the same familiar restaurant date after date won't do that. Going to the movies every month won't do it either. You need to make a concerted effort to introduce new and exciting activities into your dating repertoire. All it takes is a bit of novelty and creativity to add that little "spark" that may be missing from a relationship that has begun to feel routine and mundane. Citing a number of scientific studies, the *New York Times*

summed it up this way: "Several experiments show that novelty—
simply doing new things together as a couple—may help bring the
butterflies back, re-creating the chemical surges of early courtship."[5]

In addition to novelty, your dates need to have a healthy dose of
good, old-fashioned fun involved. This is one of the many reasons
why it's so important that you not administrate your marriage during
your dates. Sure, you could go out to dinner and discuss your budget
or your kids' report cards. You might even feel a great sense of accom-
plishment at the end of such an evening. But could you really say that
you'd had *fun* on a date like that? Probably not.

A fun date should involve plenty of opportunities for laughter.
When was the last time you enjoyed laughing together as a couple?
Once again, there are important physiological reasons why laughter
should be a key component of your marriage. Here are just a few of
the physical benefits of laughing:

- Laughter lowers your blood pressure and decreases heart
  strain.
- Laughter reduces stress hormones that constrict blood vessels
  and suppress immune activity.
- Laughter boosts your immune system and helps combat
  upper respiratory infections.
- Laughter helps tone facial muscles and nourishes the skin.
- Laughter triggers the release of endorphins—the body's natural painkillers.
- Laughter protects the stomach from forming ulcers.
- Laughter improves the body's ability to use oxygen by empty-
  ing the lungs of more air than they can take in. This results in
  a cleansing effect similar to deep breathing.

- Laughter promotes healing. Even in the most difficult times, a laugh or even a simple smile can help us feel better.
- Laughter produces a general sense of well-being.[6]

Hopefully the case is clear: By combining *novel* and *fun* activities into your dates, you'll be contributing not only to the health of your marriage but also to your individual health and well-being!

Do: Reminisce

Taking the time to *reminisce* on your date—to remember significant events as well as fun and emotional stories from everyday life—is one of the most important ways you can build intimacy. Because we've already established that your dates aren't for administrating your marriage and that they should be characterized by fun, it's probably not a good idea to spend your time reminiscing about the more tragic and terrible experiences you've had as a couple, except perhaps to reflect on how those experiences have drawn you closer and helped you grow both individually and as partners. Reminiscing is also not a time to criticize your mate or to recall his or her most embarrassing moments for the sake of a cheap laugh. It's a time to focus on the positive aspects of your experiences as a couple, whether you've been married for two years or twenty.

Reminiscing is important because it helps strengthen the bond between husband and wife and draws you closer together. If you feel as if your marriage has fallen into a rut, recalling memorable events can also provide you with a sense of hope and anticipation of similar memorable events in the future. Reminiscing can also help you recall happier times if you're currently in the midst of an unsettled or difficult season in your marriage. Finally, it can remind you of the character traits and qualities that first attracted you and your mate to each other. A time of reminiscing and sharing special memories should leave you both saying, "You know, we're actually quite good together!"

We'll share more specific thoughts on recalling good times in your marriage in the context of some specific date ideas in the next chapter. In the meantime, here are several questions you and your spouse might consider asking each other as you endeavor to evoke fond memories during the course of a date:

- What first attracted you to me?
- What was going through your mind on our first date?
- When did you know I was the person you wanted to marry?
- What were some of your impressions of the day we got engaged?
- What was your favorite part of our honeymoon?
- What was your reaction when you first found out that we were pregnant?
- What is your favorite meal that I make and why?
- What has been your most positive spiritual experience in our marriage?
- What three things have you done in our marriage that you're most proud of?
- Over the past five years, how do you think you've grown as a person?
- What would you consider to be "our" song? Why is it so meaningful to you?
- In what ways do you feel blessed in our marriage?
- What is the best gift I've ever given you? Why is it so special?

- What are some of your favorite Valentine's Day memories from our years of marriage?
- What do I do that is the biggest turn-on for you?
- What outfit of mine is your favorite? Why?
- Is there a particular church service or ceremony we've attended that was especially meaningful to you? Why?
- What is your favorite appliance or piece of furniture that we've bought together? Why?
- What is your favorite tradition that we've started? Why?
- What has been your favorite house or place we've lived and why?
- What is your favorite vacation we've taken together and why?
- What are some of your favorite date-night activities we've done together?
- What are some things I've done for you in the past that really made you feel loved?
- Where would you consider our "special place" to be? Why is it so meaningful to you?
- What's the most romantic thing I've ever done for you?
- What are some of your favorite Christmas memories during our marriage?
- What's your version of our love story?

Obviously, this list is only a beginning. Even if you've been married only a relatively short time, there are likely thousands of positive memories and experiences you could discuss and celebrate together. And we can guarantee that talking about those special times and reliving them will leave you feeling more intimate and connected by the end of your date.

Do: Select Dating Activities That Communicate Intimacy to Both of You

Dictionary.com defines *intimacy* as "a close, familiar, and usually affectionate or loving personal relationship with another person."[7] And you and your spouse likely agree that *building intimacy* is one of the primary objectives of marital dating. But here's the deal: Even with an objective definition like the one offered by Dictionary.com, the fact remains that men and women tend to define *intimacy* on very different terms.

For men, the simple act of *doing something* with their wives is enough to communicate intimacy. It doesn't have to be anything romantic on the surface. Simply playing Ping-Pong or going swimming or biking or putting a puzzle together is enough for most men to feel they have truly made a meaningful connection with their wives. Just so long as they're doing something together and enjoying it together. This doesn't mean that men are more shallow than women; it only means that they're wired differently.

The situation becomes a bit more complicated for women. While they may enjoy a wide variety of typical dating activities, whether going out to dinner or attending a play or going hiking, those shared activities are only a backdrop for what they truly need in order to experience an intimate connection with their mate: *deep, meaningful conversation.* For most women, even the most romantic candlelight dinner or sleigh ride in the snow will ring hollow if it isn't accompanied by the opportunity for meaningful conversation and interaction.

For many married couples, dating can become a frustrating experience because they tend to veer toward one extreme or the other. Either they spend all their time pursuing fun activities, leaving the wife feeling unfulfilled, or they spend all their time emoting and talking about their hopes and dreams, leaving the husband feeling unfulfilled. Again, intimacy and friendship for a man are built on a *shared activity*, but for a woman, shared activity is a backdrop for *great conversation*.

Your dates, then, need to incorporate both shared activities *and* meaningful conversation on a consistent basis. Yes, there will be some dates during which you'll spend more time "playing" and less time conversing. And there will be others that involve a great deal of discussion with less time devoted to activities. But on the whole, if you and your spouse are to feel you've made a fulfilling, intimate connection on your date, both of these need to be kept in balance.

Summing It Up

Just to review, here are the five important dos and don'ts to keep in mind as you think about planning your dates together and endeavor to make them as fun, enjoyable, and meaningful as possible:

1. *Don't administrate your marriage*—Don't talk about finances, household responsibilities, child discipline issues, or other administrative aspects of your marriage while on your date. The purpose of a date is to have fun and enjoy each other.

2. *Stay current*—Be curious about your spouse. Ask questions. Update your knowledge and deepen your understanding of each other.

3. *Try new and exciting activities*—Couples who engage in unique activities that they don't usually do experience an increase in marital satisfaction. New activities stimulate the same parts of the brain that were ignited when you were

first dating and help re-create the chemical surges of early courtship.

4. *Reminisce*—Talking about special moments or memorable events allows you to celebrate how far you've come as a couple and renews hope as you anticipate future good times together.

5. *Select dating activities that communicate intimacy to both of you*—For men, intimacy is built on a shared activity; for women, a shared activity is a backdrop to deep conversation.

There are a couple of other things to consider—issues that don't really fit in the previous list—as you prepare to embark on your joyful journey of marital dating. The first has to do with *planning* your dates. In many marriages, the wife will often invest more time, energy, and thought into the process of planning a date. Her husband may dutifully comply with whatever she has planned, but it's clear that *she* is the one primarily responsible for making date night happen.

Men, you need to be involved in planning and initiating your dates as well! Don't leave it all up to your wife. This is especially important if you're the primary breadwinner in the family. Setting aside time in your hectic schedule to be intentional about planning a date with your wife sends several very important messages to her: (1) "I'm thinking about you"; (2) "You are important to me"; and (3) "Our marriage is important to me." This goes back to the interview with President Obama that we cited earlier in the book. He essentially said that while his wife appreciates flowers and other gifts, his greatest gift to her is letting her know that he's thinking about her in the midst of life's chaos. While actually going on dates with your wife is important, it's equally important that she knows you've been thinking about her during the week, and that you're actually looking forward to spending time with her during your date. Taking the initiative to plan your dates will communicate a great deal of intimacy to your wife before the date even begins.

Finally, what is the first thing that comes to mind when you think about the concept of a date? For many people, a date is simply dinner and a movie. There's nothing wrong with this per se. An occasional movie date can be enlivening, especially if you allow time for face-to-face discussion and interaction afterward. But we'd encourage you to generally avoid making movies a major feature of your dates. Why? Because watching a movie takes your focus off each other. You're looking at a screen for two hours or more, rather than at your spouse. True, there's something romantic about sitting together in a darkened theater watching a good film, or cuddling on the couch with a DVD or Netflix. But when it comes to genuinely connecting with one another and building intimacy, there are better options available. Watching a movie is generally a passive activity rather than an engaging one that encourages you to have fun and focus on your partner.

And speaking of focusing on your partner, it should go without saying that smartphones, iPads, and other electronic devices shouldn't be allowed to intrude on your dates! It's amazing how much these modern "conveniences" have detracted from the amount of time our culture spends engaging in face-to-face interaction. We've been in restaurants and seen entire families at neighboring tables ignoring one another in favor of their electronic gadgets. The faces of Mom, Dad, and each kid are bathed in the sickly blue glow of an iPhone or portable Nintendo game system. Everyone is texting or gaming, and no one is saying a word! It's not exactly "quality" family time, is it? These families are missing out on valuable opportunities to connect and engage because they're too busy gaming, texting, checking in at work, and so on. It's really very sad, but the fact is that we've all probably been guilty of this at some point.

Don't let this happen on your dates! It's hard enough carving out the time to go out together, so don't squander that time by getting distracted by your electronic devices. Obviously, you'll want to have your smartphone along so that the babysitter will be able to contact you if any issues arise at home, and possibly to find directions to a new restaurant or other destination for your date. But other than that, keep your phone out of mind and out of sight. Date night isn't the time for texting, Facebooking, chatting with your friends, or checking your email at work.

A Word about Babysitting

We've spent many pages now talking about how to have great dates. And we're about to launch into an extended section filled with helpful and practical date-night ideas. But for many of you, there is an elephant in the room, screaming, "WAIT! WHAT ARE WE SUPPOSED TO DO WITH THE KIDS?!"

That's an excellent question! The obvious answer is, "Get a babysitter," but of course, we realize that doing so is much easier said than done, for a number of reasons. For one thing, paying a babysitter can add significantly to the cost of your date. If you're considering a particularly aggressive schedule, such as having a date once a week, you might feel you need to take out a second mortgage just to be able to pay a babysitter each time! There's also the issue of actually *finding* a quality babysitter, let alone assembling a pool of qualified candidates.

Difficult and daunting as it may be, for those of you who still have young kids at home, it's critical that you identify a few qualified, trusted individuals who can provide childcare during your dates. Let's look at a few of your options in this regard:

1. *Peer couples.* You likely know a number of other couples who are in the same stage of life as you (i.e., they're raising young children). These could be families from your church or from work, or the parents of your kids' friends at school. Identify a few trustworthy couples and approach them about the idea of creating a sort of informal babysitting co-op. How does it work? Quite simply, you offer to watch their kids on a given evening, allowing Mom and Dad to have a date night. In return, they'll watch *your* kids on another night so that you can enjoy a date of your own! The more families you get involved in your co-op, the more options you'll have when it comes time to find appropriate childcare during your dates.

There are many benefits to this approach. First, because you're trading childcare responsibilities with other couples, there's no need for money to change hands for services rendered. The out-of-pocket expense of paying for a babysitter is eliminated! Second, assuming the members of your co-op are families you already know well and have spent time with, you can feel confident trusting them with the care of your own children. Finally, creating a babysitting co-op will help you get other couples in your circle of influence involved in the date-night concept. By taking the time to watch one another's children on occasion, you're helping your friends invest in the health of their own marriages, just as they're helping you invest in the health of yours.

2. *Other friends from church, work, etc.* You probably know other families who would be willing and eager to watch your kids from time to time, even if they don't have kids of their own. This could include single adults (preferably female), married couples whose kids are older

or out of the house, retired couples, and families with responsible teenagers (again, preferably female) who could serve as babysitters. Church is a great place to find these types of families. Now don't get us wrong; we're not suggesting that the reason you should attend church is to assemble a team of babysitters. We'd be the first to affirm that church is a place for worshipping God and investing in the lives of others. Still, a wonderful "perk" of being involved in a church community is being able to call upon others within that community to come alongside you in times of need, and the need for childcare is certainly one of those occasions.

3. *Grandparents and other relatives.* In today's world, the number of families who live in close proximity to grandparents and other extended-family members has diminished considerably. Nevertheless, if you do have extended family nearby, they can be another great (and potentially free!) source of childcare during your dates. In fact, we know one couple who often takes their kids to Grandpa and Grandma's house during their dates. They sometimes offer to take the grandparents out to dinner or even pay them a little money in exchange for watching the kids. But Grandpa and Grandma always respond, "You're allowing us to spend quality time with our grandchildren—*we* should be paying *you* for this privilege!" Awww, it warms the heart, doesn't it? Now, clearly there are some grandparents who aren't physically able to care for young children for extended periods on a regular basis. You always need to be sensitive to your relatives' needs and not rely on them for childcare to the point that your kids become an imposition or an object of resentment. No one, even doting grandparents, likes to be taken advantage of. But when possible, grandparents and other extended-family members in your vicinity can be a valuable part of your larger babysitting team.

Before moving on from the subject of babysitting, let's take a closer look at a few of the things you should consider when it comes time to select a lone babysitter—not a family from your babysitting co-op and not a grandparent or relative, but a teenager who will be watching your kids alone. It can be a scary thing to entrust your little ones to the care of such an individual. When it comes to finding someone who is trustworthy and reputable, we can think of no better advice than that offered in Focus on the Family's *Complete Guide to Baby and Child Care*:

> A great deal depends upon the age of your child. During the first six months of life, it's best to leave him or her in the hands of experienced relatives or other adults. Later on you can consider using younger babysitters. In fact, some of the best babysitters in the market may turn out to be high school or middle school students. Just be certain that you've done your homework before leaving anyone in charge of your kids. If the sitter is a teenager, make sure that you're thoroughly acquainted with her, her family, and her personal background before arranging anything. If possible, have her watch your child while you're at home doing some other work. This will give you a chance to observe how she interacts with your child. You may also find some excellent sitters and have an opportunity to see them in action in the church nursery or Sunday school.
>
> It's a good idea to build a roster of trustworthy babysitters before you actually need one. Find out if the individuals you have in mind are trained and equipped to handle emergencies. In many communities, hospitals or other organizations offer short courses (including CPR training) for babysitters. Those

who have completed such a program would be excellent candidates for you to consider.

Some experts have advised against using adolescent boys as babysitters. The idea here is that the many sexual and hormonal changes occurring during the teen years may get the better of young males and lead to sexually inappropriate behavior with children while parents are out of the house. We agree that there may be room for special concern where boys are concerned, but we would [be] quick to point out that in this day and age, given the prevalence of Internet pornography and other sexually addictive materials, girls and older adults may also have problems in this area. Caution is always appropriate. The key is to be thoroughly acquainted with the person you're engaging to care for your kids—whoever he or she may be.[8]

One final note on babysitting: It goes without saying that there will be times when your scheduled babysitter has to cancel. The teenage girl you've scheduled calls at the last minute and reveals that she accidentally double-booked and can't make it. Grandpa and Grandma are feeling under the weather. The family that was scheduled to watch your kids is facing an unexpected crisis. While there may be times you'll have to cancel your date as the result of scenarios like these, don't automatically assume that it must be so. Keep a few "home date" ideas in mind for those occasions when you simply have no choice but to stay at home. After the kids are in bed, pour a glass of your favorite beverage, make a simple snack, and just spend time talking and catching up. If you're feeling really adventurous, grill some steaks, put out a nice tablecloth, light some candles, and enjoy a full romantic dinner after the kids are asleep. If it's warm, sit outside and look up at the stars. If it's cold, hunker down in front of the fireplace. When life gives you lemons, make lemonade!

Now that you have the basics down of what makes a great date, the only thing left to do is go out and put them into practice! The next chapter—which comprises the majority of this book—will provide you with some very specific date ideas to take you through an entire year of dating—or more, depending on your dating frequency. So without further ado, get ready to dive in and experience the excitement of marital dating. It's fun, it's meaningful, and it has the potential to revolutionize your relationship!

Go Forth and Date—A Year's Worth of Fun Dates

Now it's time to get down to brass tacks. You've read, and hopefully enjoyed, the first two chapters of this book, with their scientific studies and theories on why dating is so important for married couples. But let's face it; this chapter is probably the reason you wanted this book. You may appreciate knowing *why* marital dating is so important, but your primary interest is in *how* to make it happen.

You need ideas. You need inspiration. You came to the right place!

Before launching into the dates, however, let's establish a basic format. As we mentioned in the previous chapter, your dates need to include both interesting *activities* (because those communicate *intimacy* to men and also help produce dopamine and norepinephrine in both of you for that rush of excitement) and opportunities for *meaningful conversation* (which greatly communicates *intimacy* to women).

Accordingly, each of the following dates will include some introductory comments, along with some suggested activities (some of which will relate directly to the theme of your date, and some that are more general), as well as topics of conversation and questions for you to ask each other during the course of the date. Keep in mind that all of the activities, questions, and conversation topics are merely *suggestions*; they aren't hard-and-fast rules that have to be followed religiously. We encourage you to think creatively and inject your own thoughts and ideas into your dates! Feel free to amend the date templates to align with your own interests, budget considerations, and time constraints. The important thing is that your activities and discussions are consistently *fun* and *interesting*, allowing you to relax, enjoy each other's company, and connect.

Before every date, whether you're following one of the templates in this book or creating a date of your own, remember to *always act as if you're trying to get a second date*! Sometimes in marriage we forget that we need to pursue and woo our spouses. It doesn't matter whether you've been married for two weeks or twenty-five years, you still need to put your best foot forward when it comes to marital dating. So dress up a bit. Be polite and open doors. Compliment each other. Be affectionate, hold hands, cuddle, and steal kisses. And remember to protect your date night from conflict by cutting off any arguments and agreeing to talk about issues at a later time.

To make dating a habit—a regular event—we encourage you to commit to at least one date per month. Be sure to put your dates on the calendar so that you can schedule around them! If you're not intentional about setting aside the time, it likely won't happen. If your schedules and budget allow you to go on more than one date per month, so much the better.

Among the dates outlined in this chapter and the handful of special-occasion dates in chapter 4, this book contains fifty-two date ideas to get you started—one for every week of the year! If you're going for the once-a-month date plan, feel free to pick and choose from these fifty-two dates. Keep in mind that a few of them are specific to holidays on the calendar. There are date ideas for New Year's Day and

Valentine's Day early in this chapter, for example, and there are dates related to Thanksgiving, Christmas, and New Year's Eve at the end of the chapter. Otherwise, the majority of dates are general enough that they can be enjoyed at any time of year. Chapter 4 will include ideas for dates that are unique to events on your calendar but no one else's—birthdays, anniversaries, and so on.

A New Year's Date

The object of a new year is not that
we should have a new year.
It is that we should have a new soul.
—G. K. Chesterton

Let's face it, in today's world the idea of New Year's resolutions is often met with a fair amount of cynicism. Resolutions were made to be broken, right? Whether it's losing weight or starting an exercise program or reading the Bible more, most people start with the best of intentions, only to discover by mid-February (if they even make it that long) that they've gotten completely offtrack.

But what if you could work on a resolution in partnership with someone else? That's the beauty of a marriage-related New Year's resolution! In resolving to invest in your marriage, to have a monthly date night, or to set other positive goals for your relationship, you automatically have someone in your corner who is pursuing the same goals and will encourage you in your resolution. Why? Because having a stronger marriage is something couples work on *together*. It's a resolution that can be accomplished only as a *team*. A New Year's date will allow you to work together to set positive goals for yourselves (don't call them "resolutions" if you don't like the negative connotations associated with that word).

Oh, and keep in mind that you don't need to wait for a new year to start setting positive goals for your marriage. You can commit to a monthly date night *now*. You can start making an effort to encourage each other and build one another up now. Whether it's January or June, it's always a good time to start investing in your marriage.

Activity: With the idea of new goals and new beginnings fresh in your minds, consider making this date a morning affair. Rather than going out for dinner, go out for breakfast and talk about setting positive goals for your marriage while you're both still fresh and wide awake. If you're typically not a morning person, be sure breakfast is accompanied by lots of coffee or a similarly caffeinated beverage! If breakfast isn't your thing, think about doing another morning activity together, such as working out, playing racquetball, or going for a refreshing hike.

Questions: Either during your activity or afterward, discuss the following questions: What are some positive goals we can set for our marriage over the next six months? The next year? How can we work together to achieve these goals? Is there a specific area you feel God wants us to work on together, as a team, to make our marriage the best it can be?

We're a Team!

Coming together is a beginning,
staying together is progress, and
working together is success.
—Henry Ford

The best teams are passionate about their goals. If you're going to be part of a Super Bowl championship team, you need to do more than just wear the uniform. You need to be committed to your team's success. Individual players don't win games; *teams* win games. The same is true in marriage. Being married means doing more than just wearing a wedding ring. Rather, you wear the ring as a symbol of the commitment you made before God and humankind to be united as man and wife, forsaking all others. In every sense of the word, a husband and wife are a *team*.

When was the last time you and your spouse truly viewed yourselves as a team? This doesn't mean that you have to agree 100 percent of the time. But it does mean that in parenting, in church, in service to others, and in your marriage itself, you're working toward the same goals together.

The Bible reminds us that "the body is a unit, though it is made up of many parts; and though all its parts are many, they form one body. So it is with Christ" (1 Corinthians 12:12). And so it is with your marriage. Each of you brings your own personality, experiences, and viewpoints to the table, but at the end of the day, you work together as a single unit. That's the beauty of marital teamwork!

Activity: Here's a chance to have some real fun working as a team! Think of some invigorating, team-based activities that you and your spouse can work on together. Although date night should typically be reserved for couple time, this might be an occasion to get some other friends involved. Here are just a few possibilities:

- Go to a karaoke club and sing a duet together. Wow the crowd as you belt out your favorite torch song!
- Take some ballroom dancing lessons, or if you'd rather just wing it, go find a place that offers ballroom dancing and cut a rug together. This is an activity that definitely requires team-work. Each person has a part to play. One leads; the other follows. If one partner makes a mistake, the other can help correct it and get back on rhythm or back on course. When both partners are working together in perfect harmony, the dance can be a beautiful thing.
- Host a game night with some other married couples. Rather than resorting to the typical guys-versus-gals model, play games in which each married couple works together as a team. Brainstorm with your partner, strategize, and pool your resources. Win or lose, you'll experience the joy and satisfaction of working *together*.

Questions: What are some famous teams you admire? (*Note:* We're not just talking sports teams here, although there are certainly some inspiring examples in that category. But be sure to include other famous teams, such as George Burns and Gracie Allen, or Richard and Karen Carpenter, or Greg and Erin Smalley, or . . . well, you get the idea.) What about these famous teams is inspiring? What makes them work well together? What are some practical steps we can take to ensure that we're always working as a team?

There's Always Something More to Learn

The cure for boredom is curiosity.
There is no cure for curiosity.
—Dorothy Parker

This is an important theme we've already addressed earlier in the book: there is *always* something new to learn about your spouse. Always. No matter how long you've been married, no matter how much you think you know about the person you married, you haven't even scratched the surface. Human beings are complex. They change over time. The opinions and viewpoints your spouse held when you first got married may have completely evolved by now, in subtle and not-so-subtle ways (remember the Diet Coke story?).

The goal in marriage, then, is not to learn everything there is to learn about your spouse. We've already established that it isn't possible. It's important, however, to continually be a *student* of your spouse. This is a lifelong process. You may never know everything there is to know, but it's important to update your knowledge at every opportunity. That same sense of discovery you had during your time of premarital dating is possible now. You just need to remain curious!

Activity: During this date, what you say—what you discuss— may be more important than the activity itself. So feel free to engage in a typical dating activity, such as going out for a nice dinner or playing a round of miniature golf or just taking a romantic walk in the park. On the other hand, you may consider creating an activity that stimulates your curiosity. For example, you could plan your date around the famous ice-breaker game Two Truths and a Lie. Each of you could write down three statements about yourself, two of which are true and one of which isn't. Then during your date, exchange your statements and see if your spouse can figure out which statement about you isn't true. You'll obviously have to dig a bit deeper and be a bit more creative than you would if you were playing the same game with a group of strangers or casual acquaintances.

Of course, under normal circumstances we wouldn't advocate that you and your spouse lie to each other! If the thought of "lying" in this way, even in the name of good fun, is uncomfortable to you, simply create a quiz about yourself that your spouse can answer during the date. You'd be surprised how challenging such an activity can be, even with seemingly obvious questions like "What is my favorite food?" "What is my favorite movie?" or "What is my favorite color?" See how many questions your spouse can answer before he or she gets tripped up! The idea here isn't to humiliate your spouse or berate him or her for not knowing basic information but to simply have fun rediscovering each other and relearning information you may have taken for granted.

Questions: After completing the Two Truths and a Lie game or taking your quiz, discuss the following questions: What one thing did you learn about me tonight that you didn't know before? What are some practical steps we can take to stay current with each other? What does it mean to you to be a student of me?

Random Acts of Kindness

Three things in human life are important:
the first is to be kind; the second is to be kind;
and the third is to be kind.

—Henry James

Do you make an effort to be kind to each other, simply for the sake of being kind? Married couples often fall into the routine of doing nice things for one another only when it's absolutely necessary or, even worse, as a way of coercing their partner into something. For example, there's nothing wrong with giving your wife flowers on her birthday, but let's face it; that's what is expected of you. Husbands, when was the last time you gave your wife flowers "just because"? Or wives, have you ever put on a sexy negligee and invited your husband to bed with the caveat that this sexual interlude will be possible only if he fixes the leaky faucet that he's been promising to fix for weeks? Or have you ever rewarded him with sex as *payment* for fixing the leaky faucet? That's not kindness. It's more of a business arrangement.

The type of kindness we have in mind is the self-sacrificing, giving, "just because I love you" type of kindness that isn't coercive and doesn't expect something in return. These don't have to be huge, expensive "events." They can be simple everyday activities that convey your love and appreciation to your spouse. It might be helping put the kids to bed—or even handling the bedtime routine all by yourself without being asked to do so—even though that's typically your spouse's responsibility. It might be calling to remind your spouse that you're praying for him or her—or even praying together over the phone—on a day when an important meeting is taking place at work. In marriage, the most important acts of kindness are those un-prompted, simple gestures of love that say, "I love you, I'm thinking about you, and I care about you" on a daily basis.

Activity: Go out for dinner and then pick another fun date activity—perhaps bowling or visiting an amusement park or an arcade. Over the course of the date, make every effort to be extra thoughtful and courteous toward your spouse. Don't take him or her for granted. Enjoy the experience of simply being kind to each other. Don't be dis-ingenuous about it, but don't be afraid to lay it on thick either. Think of things that would be genuinely helpful to your spouse—simple things that make him or her feel loved and appreciated—and then do them.

Questions: After your activity is over, go somewhere quiet and enjoy a time of conversing and connecting. Discuss the following questions: What are some of the "little things" I did for you on our date that you appreciated? Over the course of a typical week, how do I demonstrate my love for you? What else can I do in the future?

Be sure to keep your answers uplifting and affirming. The idea isn't to criticize your spouse in the areas where he or she is falling short. The goal is to affirm what he or she is already doing, to exchange ideas, and to offer helpful suggestions for the future.

The Blessing

Nothing tears down a marriage or family
like criticism, and nothing builds and restores
it like words of encouragement and praise.
—Dr. Steve Stephens,
The Wounded Woman

Since it was first published in 1990, millions of readers have been impacted by Dr. John Trent and Dr. Gary Smalley's book *The Blessing*. (A shout-out to Greg's dad!) Based on numerous examples in Scripture, including those involving God the Father blessing His children, "the blessing" includes five elements:[1]

1. *Meaningful and appropriate touch.* This is key to communicating warmth, acceptance, and affirmation.

2. *Spoken words.* To see the blessing grow in someone's life, "we need to verbalize our message."[2] Blessing-filled *words*—both spoken and written—communicate genuine acceptance.

3. *Expressing high value.* In blessing one of his sons, Isaac said, "Ah, the smell of my son is like the smell of a field that the LORD has blessed" (Genesis 27:27). "Word pictures are a powerful way of communicating acceptance."[3]

4. *Picturing a special future.* Throughout Scripture, God "goes to great lengths to assure us of our present relationship with Him and of the ocean full of blessings in store for us as His children."[4] We need to picture just such a special future for our loved ones if we are serious about giving them our blessing.

5. *An active commitment.* "Words alone cannot communicate
the blessing; they need to be backed with a commitment to
do everything possible to help the one blessed be successful."[5]

We might think of the blessing as something communicated exclusively from parent to child, but the fact is that these elements are an important part of the marital relationship as well. Is touching—both sexual and nonsexual—an important part of your relationship? Do you use words and *word pictures* to let your spouse know that he or she is valued? Do you know what it means to picture a special future for your spouse by speaking positively and encouraging your spouse in his or her goals? And finally, do you demonstrate an active commitment to your spouse by choosing to love him or her even during those times when you disagree and you're facing stress and crisis? Incorporating the blessing into your marriage can revolutionize your relationship!

Activity: If you're not familiar with the concept of the blessing, track down a copy of the original book, or better yet, find *The Gift of the Blessing*,[6] which includes a chapter written exclusively with married couples in mind. If possible, read the relevant sections before your date so you'll be familiar with the concepts by the time your date night arrives. Then, either over dinner or at your favorite coffee shop, or in another quiet location, host your own two-person Blessing Discussion Group.

Questions: As you discuss incorporating the blessing into your marriage, be sure to address the following questions: Did you feel blessed by your parents? Why or why not? What do I do that blesses you? How can we further incorporate the five elements of the blessing into our marriage?

(*Note:* There is certainly a time and a place to talk about introducing the concepts of *The Blessing* into your family, especially when it comes to your relationships with your children. Blessing your kids is one of the most important things you can do! However, for the purposes of date night, try to focus your conversation exclusively on ways to implement the blessing into your marriage, and then commit to making it part of your parenting at a later time.)

A Valentine's Day Date

*I think that men know how to romance a woman,
and most do it well, at least for a time, otherwise
women wouldn't marry them. The problem is that
most of them begin to rest on their laurels.*

—Nicholas Sparks

Ah, Valentine's Day. It's a holiday that can paralyze men with the fear of forgetting it or not living up to expectations and making women swoon with the romantic possibilities it represents. Even if you haven't had a strong track record in marital dating over the years, chances are you've made an exception or two on Valentine's Day. Our culture makes it easy to celebrate this holiday devoted to romantic love. Its history spans centuries and includes at least three different saints named Valentine or Valentinus, as well as dramatic accounts of the church's attempts to transform pagan ceremonies into Christian observances. But let's face it: In its modern incarnation, Valentine's Day is essentially a shopping tradition kept alive by florists and greeting-card and candy companies. (Considering the fact that Valentine chocolates start appearing on store shelves literally the day after Christmas, it's amazing that so many men still fail to remember Valentine's Day after the nearly two months of marketing that precede it!)

Now, don't get us wrong. We're not anti–Valentine's Day. Any holiday that encourages couples to turn toward each other and devote attention to the romantic aspects of their relationship is fine by us.

However, when it comes to married couples, Valentine's Day can create a problem for a couple of reasons. First, thriving relationships need far more than one day per year devoted to expressions of romantic love. If you're saving all your hugs and kisses and flowers and romantic gestures for February 14th, while the rest of the year is just the "same old, same old," your relationship likely won't survive. It's as simple as that. Your spouse needs to be reminded, reassured, and encouraged in your love for him or her on a regular and consistent basis, all year, every year.

Second, Valentine's Day is a concern because of the sheer materialism of the day. Christmas has become this way as well. When it comes to Valentine's Day, our culture encourages us to buy *bigger* bouquets, *bigger* stuffed bears, *bigger* boxes of chocolate, and perhaps *smaller*, skimpier, and more shocking lingerie! Now, there's nothing inherently wrong with flowers, teddy bears, chocolates, or sexy lingerie. Men, however, often feel compelled to purchase these items not out of genuine love and affection for their wives but out of a desire to outdo other guys. Sometimes wives can contribute to this problem as well by comparing the exorbitant and extravagant lengths their husbands have gone to to make Valentine's Day "special." In reality, though, it isn't about expressing genuine love and care for your spouse; it's about buying stuff, under compulsion, to create the illusion of intimacy. But if you've failed to pursue and foster relational intimacy with your spouse on a regular basis *throughout the year*, an oversized teddy bear on February 14th isn't going to fix the problem.

Activity: Again, we're not anti–Valentine's Day. If a romantic dinner on February 14th is your annual tradition, by all means, go for it! However, you might also consider doing something outside the norm. While everyone *else* is dining by candlelight, perhaps the two of you could play laser tag or go fishing! Who says activities like these can't be romantic? It all depends on your attitude. Sometimes doing something new, exciting, and unexpected can create more vivid memories than repeating the same thing year after year. And don't worry, you can still cap off the evening by returning home and breaking out the sexy lingerie!

Questions: Because Valentine's Day is an annual event, it presents a great opportunity for reminiscing. Either during your activity or in a quiet location afterward, take some time to remember and reflect upon your previous Valentine's Days together. Discuss the following questions: Do you remember our first Valentine's Day together? What did we do last year for Valentine's Day? Let's see if we can make a list, by year, of all our Valentine's Day dates up to this point.

Shared Interests

Friendship . . . is born at the moment when
one [person] says to another, "What! You too?
I thought that no one but myself . . ."
—C. S. Lewis, *The Four Loves*

It's a common theme for many married couples. He likes to do "guy stuff" like playing sports, collecting baseball cards, or going hunting. She likes "girly stuff" like scrapbooking, sewing, or blogging about bargains. When it comes to movies, he's a *Saving Private Ryan* fan, while she loves any film with the phrase "based on the novel by Jane Austen" in the credits. Certainly, some of these activities speak to the innate differences between males and females. There's nothing wrong with husbands and wives having different likes and dislikes based on their unique personalities, talents, and experiences. It would be a serious mistake, however, for couples to assume that every moment of free time should be relegated to "his interests" and "her interests," and never the twain shall meet.

Having common hobbies can help couples deepen their sense of intimacy, connection, and especially *friendship*. When was the last time you thought about your spouse as your friend—someone you enjoy spending time with and with whom you can engage in mutually satisfying pursuits? If husbands and wives have a firm grasp of their roles as partners, lovers, or parents but fail to understand what it means to be friends, they're missing out on a key component of marriage. The Bible places the concept of friendship front and center in King Solomon's depiction of romantic love: "This is my lover, this [is] my *friend*" (Song of Songs 5:16).

Activity: Choosing a new restaurant is a fantastic way for husbands and wives to develop a common interest. Find a restaurant or a type of cuisine that *neither* of you has tried before. You'll experience something new together for the first time. And who knows? You both just might like it! If you have time prior to your date, google "date-night ideas," "hobbies for married couples," or a similar phrase to identify potential activities that you might enjoy together. The idea is not only to select a new and exciting activity for your date but also to identify a hobby or pastime the two of you, as a couple, can return to again and again as a shared interest. If your first attempt isn't a success (i.e., if one or both of you feel that your chosen activity isn't the thrilling experience you thought it would be), try again with a new activity on another date night. Keep trying until you've found something that works for both of you! The possibilities are endless, but here are just a few activities you might consider:

- Cycling
- Bird watching
- Coauthoring a blog
- Collecting antiques or artwork
- Composing music together or jamming on instruments
- Photography
- Clay modeling or pottery
- Scuba diving
- Horseback riding
- Learning a form of self-defense
- "Treasure hunting" with a metal detector
- Gardening or landscaping

- Cooking
- Volunteering at church or with a local social-service agency

Questions: After your activity, discuss the following questions: What were some of your favorite hobbies as a child? Have any of those hobbies retained your interest as an adult? What are some of the key things that make your favorite hobbies enjoyable? Do you prefer activities that are more physical in nature, or those that provide a mental challenge? What hobby would you pursue if time and money weren't factors?

The final, and most important, question for you to discuss is this: Did both of you truly enjoy your shared experience? Remember, the purpose of a shared interest isn't to let one spouse be a martyr for the sake of the other, suffering through something that he or she truly doesn't enjoy, but to identify and cultivate activities that both spouses genuinely enjoy doing together.

Windshield Time!

Stop worrying about the potholes in
the road and celebrate the journey.
—attributed to Barbara Hoffman

According to a 2009 Department of Transportation survey, the average adult spent almost a *full hour* in the car every day.[7] We can all relate to that, right? Whether it's the daily commute to and from work, a hectic schedule of taxiing kids to school and other activities, or simply running errands, driving is a significant part of our everyday experience.

The question is, *How do you use that time?* Is driving simply a chore—a means of getting from point A to point B? It doesn't have to be that way. Rather than allowing drive time to become just another part of the daily grind, consider making it an opportunity to connect with those you love. You don't have to wait for family devotions or some other preplanned event to connect with your kids. You can have meaningful conversations and make genuine connections during the hour or more every day that you spend in the car with them.

The same is true for you and your spouse. It's important, while you're in the car together, to embrace the opportunity to connect through conversation. It's about *enjoying* the drive rather than simply getting through it. It's called "windshield time." You may be simply making a quick trip to the grocery store. But those few moments in the car—something that seems so basic and routine—represent an opportunity for you and your spouse to share your feelings and connect. That's windshield time!

Think back to your most recent date. Did you talk about anything meaningful in the car on the way to dinner, or were you simply in a hurry to get to the restaurant? After dinner, did you share anything special with each other when you were en route from dinner to your next destination? Whether it's your regular date or any other time you and your spouse spend together in the car . . . *it's not just about the destination; it's about the journey!*

Activity: Most often, windshield time will take place during the course of your daily routine, such as running errands or picking up the kids from school. However, to help you get more comfortable with the idea of connecting with your spouse while driving, the majority of this date will be spent in your car. Just drive and enjoy having the extra time to connect with each other. Here are some ideas:

- Don't be afraid to venture outside the city limits. Drive to a neighboring city for dinner.
- Are there any scenic byways in your area? Are there out-of-the-way back roads known for their sightseeing potential? Explore the world around you.
- If you'll be driving after dark, find out whether there are any roads that overlook the city lights. There's nothing like taking in a romantic cityscape!
- Even if you'd rather stay close to town, there are likely places nearby that you might enjoy seeing from inside your car—a famous building, a city landmark, or a historic neighborhood.

Questions: Remember, the purpose of windshield time is to learn how to connect with meaningful conversation while you're in the car, not to drive for driving's sake. Windshield time is a chance to invest in your spouse. This is important on your date, of course, but it's especially critical during those times in the car that might otherwise seem routine and mundane. Here are some possible questions to discuss:

- What are some ways I can show you I'm interested in you and want to know you better?
- What are some ways I can more effectively communicate that I love you?
- Did you go on family drives as a child? How did that time make you feel?
- Out of all the date nights we've experienced together thus far, which one has been your favorite? Why?

When we first started putting these principles into practice in our own relationship, I (Greg) knew that I needed to start asking Erin questions, but I didn't really know how to go about it in a meaningful way. So I asked Erin directly, "What are some questions I could ask you on a regular basis that would show you I'm trying to stay current and update my knowledge of you?" Erin suggested I try these questions:

- How are you feeling emotionally?
- How are things going between you and the kids?
- How are things going between you and your girlfriends?
- What is one thing God has been teaching you lately?

Passion

> *Boys and girls in America have such a sad time*
> *together; sophistication demands that they submit*
> *to sex immediately without proper preliminary*
> *talk. Not courting talk—real straight talk about*
> *souls, for life is holy and every moment is precious.*
> —Jack Kerouac, *On the Road*

Even beat poet Jack Kerouac understood that human sexuality is special—and sacred. It involves not only the body but the soul. It represents the pinnacle of human connection and is not to be taken lightly.

If that's the case, then why is it so difficult for married couples to enjoy a thriving sexual relationship as the years go by? We may believe in our heads that sex with our spouse is important, but it's incredibly difficult to give it the priority it deserves. When we do find the time, the experience is often routine and mundane—just another item to check off the list. One study found that due to jobs, kids, hobbies, family responsibilities, and other factors, the average married couple spends just *four minutes a day* alone together.[8] Four minutes! That's barely enough time to say hello, let alone engage in meaningful physical intimacy.

And that's what this date is all about—*intimacy*, of which sex is only one expression. As we mentioned earlier, Dictionary.com defines *intimacy* as "a close, familiar, and usually affectionate or loving personal relationship with another person or group." Did you catch that? Closeness. Familiarity. Affection. Love. Isn't that what marriage is all about? This date is not only about sex (although there's nothing wrong with that!); it's about how to foster greater intimacy with each other, even in the face of the myriad responsibilities and distractions that confront you on a daily basis.

Activity: Order in and enjoy a great meal and conversation in the comfort of your own home. Light some candles and put out a table-cloth, even if you'll only be eating out of your to-go containers. Light candles in the bedroom, the living room, and other areas where you'll be spending time as well. Break out your wedding album or video and reminisce about the special events of that day. Celebrate the journey that has brought you from that day to today. Put on some romantic music. Whether it's Barry White or Enya or instrumental praise, find something that will help set a relaxed, romantic mood. Even though you won't be leaving the house, be sure to put effort into looking attractive for your spouse.

Questions: Asking each other questions—that's not very sexy, is it? It certainly can be! Obviously, male-female relationships are about more than physical attraction. But that doesn't mean physical attraction is a bad thing! Take turns talking with your spouse about the physical features you find particularly appealing in him or her. Be specific! And what about nonphysical characteristics? Are you attracted to your spouse's sense of humor? Intellect? Compassionate heart? Let him or her know!

Be sure to flavor these conversations with plenty of cuddling, kissing, and so on. Here are some ideas to get you started:

- Engage in nonsexual touching, such as back rubs and foot massages. Enjoy being in close physical proximity without feeling the need to jump right into the "main event."

- As the evening has progressed, hopefully you and your spouse have begun to feel closer and more connected. This closeness—this *intimacy*—has likely produced in both of you a desire to connect sexually. That's a wonderful gift! But it's possible that at this point in your marriage, you've settled into a comfortable and predictable sexual routine. There's nothing wrong with that, just as there's nothing wrong with driving the same route to work every day. Nevertheless, adding some excitement to your sex life can be a wonderful thing. As you and your spouse enter this phase of the evening, ask yourselves the following questions: Is there anything specific we can do to "spice up" our sex life and add some variety? How can I be more giving toward you during sex?

- Keep in mind that the idea isn't to engage in activities that are uncomfortable for either partner. If you try something new (or that hasn't been a part of your repertoire for a while), make sure it's mutually agreed upon and edifying to both partners.

- The cliché is that after sex, the man will roll over and go to sleep while the woman lies awake, wishing for additional time to cuddle, talk, and connect. Husbands, here's your chance to shatter that stereotype! Spend some additional time connecting emotionally and physically with your wife.

I Cherish You

Where your treasure is,
there your heart will be also.
—Matthew 6:21

"Absence makes the heart grow fonder." "Familiarity breeds contempt." While usually spoken in jest, these phrases suggest that the longer two people stay together, the more likely it is they'll become bored with each other and take one another for granted. If you want to maintain a vibrant marriage, you need to take steps to counteract this tendency. You can do this by learning to *cherish* your mate.

According to *Merriam-Webster* online dictionary, *cherish* means "to hold dear,"[9] to regard someone or something as a treasure. This comes naturally to those who are caught up in the first flush of youthful romantic love. But feelings can fade over time, and when that happens, cherishing can survive and thrive only if it graduates to a higher level. It needs to be lifted out of the realm of mere emotion and transformed into a steady, consistent attitude. It has to become an intentional act of the will. How is this accomplished? The answer is simple: by *remembering*.

Thriving couples can treasure and honor each other by keeping a conscious account of the things they value about their relationship. This is most effectively achieved by preserving precious memories and reminders in a tangible, physical way—for example, by keeping a journal or writing down a list of the qualities you love and admire most in your spouse (and sharing it with him or her as opportunities arise).

It's also important to take time out to celebrate anniversaries and other significant marital milestones. These occasions can be enhanced by exchanging special gifts—for example, a ring or a pendant—intended to commemorate meaningful events in a couple's life.

I (Greg) saw the beauty of the "cherish list" in action a few years ago when Erin and I spent Thanksgiving at my parents' home in Branson, Missouri. At one point, my folks got into a huge argument. (Yes, it happens in the elder Smalley household. One of the things I admire about my parents' marriage is that they don't claim to have a "perfect" relationship, and they're not afraid to disagree.) This particular disagreement was a doozy, to the point that my folks retired to opposite ends of the house for a while. I ventured into my dad's study later to see how he was doing. I found him sitting at his computer and assumed he was catching up on the news or weather. Instead, he was reading a document he had created called "Why Norma Is So Valuable" (that's my mom's name). The list contained literally hundreds of words and phrases describing my mom's value. It was astonishing!

I asked him about it, and he said, "Years ago I started a list of reasons why your mom is so valuable. When I'm upset with her or when we've had a fight, instead of sitting here thinking about how hurt or frustrated I am, I make myself read through this list. The more I read, the faster I realize that you have an amazing mom." That's the power of cherishing your mate!

Activity: *Before* your date, each of you should take some time alone to make a list of the things you value about your spouse. Include his or her personality traits, character qualities, spirituality, caring behaviors, accomplishments, and even physical characteristics. Write them down and take the list with you on your date. Then, over dinner or in a quiet location, share your cherish lists with each other. Don't simply hand your list to your spouse and expect him or her to read it in silence. Instead, actually *read* your list aloud. Feel free to add additional details to what is written on the page. For example, if you listed "compassion" as one of the things you cherish about your mate, cite a specific example of a time you observed him or her being compassionate. Receiving those words of affirmation and love in both written and verbal forms will be much more meaningful to your spouse.

After you've shared your list, give it to your spouse and, if time allows, consider going to a scrapbook or craft store to get some stickers or even picture frames to adorn your lists. Keeping the list you've been given in a wallet or purse, on the nightstand, or in another easily seen location will remind you regularly of the reasons your spouse cherishes you.

Questions: After you've exchanged your cherish lists, answer the following questions: What was your favorite part of the evening? What is one thing you learned about me tonight that you didn't know before? What is one way I can let you know I cherish you during the coming week?

Finally, remember that the cherish list you created wasn't just for your spouse's benefit; it's a way to help *you* be intentional about honoring and cherishing your mate.

I Feel Loved When You . . .

It's not who I am underneath,
but what I do that defines me.
—Batman, in *Batman Begins*

Batman knows that being a superhero involves more than just talking about the importance of truth and justice. It's not simply believing in the right things. At some point, those beliefs and feelings have to translate into something tangible. This principle applies to marriage as well. You may have deep feelings of love for your spouse in your heart, and you may even express those feelings in words on a regular basis. But at some point, those feelings need to be put into *action*!

To express your love in tangible ways is to *nourish* your spouse. It's closely related to *cherishing*. Both disciplines are drawn from the apostle Paul's letter to the church at Ephesus, when he wrote, "No one ever hated his own flesh, but *nourishes* and *cherishes* it, just as Christ also does the church" (Ephesians 5:29, NASB). "Cherishing," as described in the previous date, is an *attitude* that involves recognizing your mate's inherent value. "Nourishing," on the other hand, is an *action* in which you treat your spouse in ways that show you value him or her.

During the previous date, you developed a list of the traits and characteristics you admire about your spouse and shared that list with him or her. Now you're going to breathe life into those thoughts and emotions and *nourish* each other.

I (Greg) have an especially gripping illustration about feeling loved. I'm just glad I lived to tell the tale. One early morning, Erin woke me up and said that she thought she heard a noise outside our house—a car idling. Although this would have been impossible to hear (our house was set way off the road), Erin begged me to take a quick look around. So I got out of bed and cautiously crept around the house, checking all the doors and windows. As I headed back to our bedroom, I turned on the hall light to find my way. I saw a lump on Erin's side of the bed, but what I didn't know was that it was made up of several pillows she had strategically placed there. She was actually hiding on the floor on my side of the bed! As I rounded the end of the bed, Erin screamed a horror-movie scream and pulled me down! For a moment I thought the mysterious idling-car man was attacking me. And so I yelled to Erin, "I love you, and I'll see you in heaven!" It was at that moment I realized my attacker was Erin herself.

To be completely honest, after I got over the initial shock of it all, I realized that I had never felt so loved in all my life. I love it when Erin is being playful and we're laughing together. The real relational benefit of humor is that it opens your heart. It's impossible to have a closed heart and laugh at the same time. A wise man once declared, "Laughter opens your heart and soothes your soul."[10]

Activity: Either over dinner or in a quiet location, talk about ways you can nourish each other spiritually, emotionally, and physically. Remember, this isn't a time to criticize your partner for his or her shortcomings, but rather to share helpful information that will help you both feel more connected, more intimate. Get a pen and paper and write down your ideas, starting with the phrase "I feel loved when you . . ." For example, I feel loved when you . . .

pray with me and share a deep faith.

provide positive affirmation.

express gratitude.

listen and validate my feelings.

spend time with me.

act curious about me.

provide affection.

serve me in ways that are meaningful to me.

have fun and laugh with me.

Once you've completed your lists, exchange them and talk about them. If there's time, you might engage in a simple activity that will help you put the idea of nourishing into practice. For example:

- Go bowling and be sure to provide each other with lots of positive affirmation (even if your spouse's ball continually ends up in the gutter!).
- Go to a movie and use the time as an opportunity to be affectionate—hold hands, put your arm around your wife, etc.
- Go to a secluded location, even if just sitting in the car, and pray together. Make an effort to connect on a spiritual level.

Questions: After your activity, discuss the following questions: What was your favorite part of the evening? What was one thing you learned about me on our date? What are some other ways I can nourish you in the days and weeks ahead?

Holy

> *If God had the gospel of Jesus's salvation in mind*
> *when he established marriage, then marriage only*
> *"works" to the degree that [it] approximates the*
> *pattern of God's self-giving love in Christ.*
> —Timothy Keller, *The Meaning of Marriage*

Do you and your spouse feel as if you're growing together spiritually? Many couples not only struggle to build physical, emotional, and relational intimacy in their marriages (hence the need for regular date nights!), but they also discover that it's tough to be *spiritually* intimate with each other. The reasons for this are similar to the reasons why it's tough to build intimacy in other areas: limited time; a too-busy lifestyle; the demands of childrearing, career, and, yes, even church. Most of us struggle to have just a few minutes of personal prayer and Bible reading on a regular basis, let alone find time to pray or study Scripture with our spouses! Like cultivating romance with your beloved, fostering spiritual growth—both individually and in your marriage—takes discipline and intentionality. It won't just happen.

It's worth noting that in some marriages, husband and wife come from very different spiritual backgrounds and perspectives. She might hail from a family that attended a charismatic church, spoke in tongues, and shouted "Hallelujah!" at every opportunity. His family, while no less "saved," may have been very stoic, introspective, and reserved about spiritual matters. Hopefully couples address and reconcile these types of spiritual differences prior to marriage, perhaps in the context of premarital counseling. Still other couples face even greater spiritual barriers, such as when one spouse has little to no interest in spiritual matters, while the other desires regular church attendance and Bible study. These are very real challenges, but they lie beyond the scope of this book. If you're in this position, we'd recommend Lee Strobel's book *Surviving a Spiritual Mismatch in Marriage.*[11]

For the purposes of this date, we'll assume that you and your spouse are roughly in the same ballpark when it comes to your Christian walk. The goal of this date will be to help you "encourage one another—and all the more as you see the Day approaching" (Hebrews 10:25).

For more insights into growing spiritually as a couple, we'd recommend Dennis and Barbara Rainey's excellent book *Moments with You.*[12]

Activity: Let's face it, all of us as Christians can be guilty of compartmentalizing our faith. We do "church stuff" on Sunday and "regular stuff" the rest of the week. But while corporate worship is important, in reality we're *always* in God's presence, whether we're singing hymns in a congregation or washing the dishes at home. The same is true of date night. Do you view your dates as opportunities to invite God into your activities—and not just with a quick "Thank You, Lord, for this food" before dinner? Your dates represent a wonderful opportunity for you to dig deep and connect spiritually as a couple. For this date, consider one of the following activities to help direct your thoughts heavenward:

- Attend a Christian concert.
- Visit a museum or exhibit dedicated to religious art, Christian iconography, or biblical history.

- Go for a hike and consider God's handiwork in nature.
- Reach out to someone in Jesus' name—volunteer at a soup kitchen or a homeless shelter.

Questions: The real meat of this date will become evident in your discussion. After your activity, explore some of the following questions: How would you share your testimony with me if I were a new acquaintance? What one person in your life has been most influential in shaping your view of God? How can I pray for you? What have you been learning during your times of personal prayer and Scripture reading? What recent sermons have impacted you at church?

Most important, ask yourselves this: *How can we continue to help each other grow spiritually on a regular basis?* The purpose of this date isn't to have a one-time spiritual discussion and then return to your regular routine. It's about making spiritual intimacy a regular feature of your marriage. Create a game plan for how you can both devote regular, consistent time to growing *together* spiritually, as well as encouraging and building each other up (see 1 Thessalonians 5:11). This may be a lot to tackle in one date, so don't hesitate to spread the discussion over two or three dates—whatever it takes. At the end of your date, be sure to pray together, asking the Lord for encouragement, determination, and resolve as you seek to foster deeper spiritual intimacy.

Here are a few general suggestions:

- Commit to praying together, not just with the kids at meals and bedtime, but just the two of you—perhaps briefly in the morning when you wake up or at night before you go to sleep.
- Read Scripture together. Take turns reading aloud.
- Set aside a regular time to study a devotional book together.

- Keep each other regularly updated with personal prayer requests. Use a notebook or even text your requests to each other.

Speaking of texts, use them, along with phone calls and emails, to send encouraging Scriptures to each other, along with other uplifting messages, even something as simple as "I love you and I'm praying for you today."

Remember When . . .

Sweet memories, of holding hands and red
bouquets, of twilight trimmed in purple haze,
and laughing eyes and simple ways . . .
— "Memories," performed by Elvis Presley

We've already established that one of the best ways for couples to build intimacy is through *reminiscing*. Remembering and celebrating special times in your relationship are very important. Often when we think of reminiscing, we tend to frame it in the context of remembering those really *big* events from marriage—our wedding day, the birth of a child, a dream vacation, and so on. There's certainly value and merit in recalling these major events, some of which have been literally life changing.

But what about the little things? What about those everyday occasions in our married and family lives that aren't accompanied by a great deal of sparkle and fanfare? Sometimes, the sweetest, most tender memories are those that happened during unplanned moments that may seem unremarkable to the casual observer. Think about some of those times in your own marriage: doing the dishes or other household chores together, working in the garden together, or just sitting on the front step on warm summer evenings watching the neighborhood wind down. These are typical daily occurrences, but when viewed from the present looking back, they can carry an added sense of peace and connection between you and your spouse.

Embrace this date as an opportunity for you and your spouse to remember some of your happiest times together, whether big events or simple everyday activities. As C. S. Lewis wrote, "A pleasure is full grown only when it is remembered."[13]

Activity: We live in a mobile society, so statistically, the chances aren't great that you still live near the old haunts you visited during your dating or courtship. Some couples move several times within their first few years of marriage! Nevertheless, if you *do* still have access to some of the places you frequented during the early years of your relationship, why don't you visit them again? And even if you've moved away, you can improvise. Maybe you had a favorite coffee shop in Des Moines when you first met during your college years. Now that you live in Sacramento, see if you can find a similar coffee shop that will help you relive that experience.

Questions: In chapter 2 we shared a lengthy list of questions to help you reminisce on your dates. This would be a great time to pull out that list and select a few items for discussion! In addition, consider the following questions: What are some favorite things we used to do as a couple in the early days of our marriage? Can we start doing some of those things again, even with the realities of our busier lifestyle? Name two special memories you cherish that have nothing to do with the big events of your relationship (the wedding, childbirth, etc.). Why are those memories so special to you?

Laugh with Me

*Among those whom I like or admire, I can find
no common denominator, but among those
whom I love, I can; all of them make me laugh.*
—W. H. Auden

A few years ago, we were teaching at a marriage retreat in Sugarcreek, Ohio. The retreat coordinator, Beau, was the family pastor from a nearby church. He had a great sense of humor, and we instantly connected with him. One of the things we discovered was Beau's love of ice cream. But he didn't love just any brand of ice cream; he was partial to a local brand that memorialized a little girl who had lost her life to cancer. Elena's Blueberry Pie ice cream was *delicious*, to say the least.

Beau was indulging in a pint but had left it unattended for a moment. So I (Erin) found a couple rolls of Smarties, those sour candies that come rolled together in a little plastic wrapper. I emptied two packages into Beau's Blueberry Pie ice cream and then stirred it up so he wouldn't notice. When Beau returned, he took a big bite of his treasured ice cream. I wish you could have seen his face. As soon as he crunched into one of the Smarties, his face contorted, looking as if he'd just eaten a poison apple. He instantly spit out the bite and grabbed a big glass of water. A crowd gathered around him to make sure he wasn't having a heart attack or going into anaphylactic shock. We roared with laughter. What I didn't know is that Beau absolutely despises Smarties. It was the perfect prank, but Beau would seek his revenge.

The next morning, we had finished packing our suitcases and

were wheeling our luggage out of the hotel room. I (Greg) was dragging both large suitcases, so I wasn't paying attention. As I headed out the door, my face hit something, and I bounced back into the room. In that instant I couldn't make sense of what was happening. It was as if I had run into an invisible force field. I was looking straight ahead, but there was something blocking me from exiting the room. It took me several seconds to realize that someone had stretched several large sheets of plastic wrap across our doorway. And the plastic was drawn so tight that you literally couldn't even tell it was there. Beau! He had played his hand, and I was the unlucky recipient of his revenge prank. Between Erin and Beau, I felt as though I were living in a frat house.

Do you ever wonder why so many personal ads, from both men and women, seek a partner with a good sense of humor, or someone who loves to laugh? Because laughter is attractive! This is true at the beginning of a relationship, and it's true after years of marriage. An article in *Scientific American* notes that "when seeking a mate, men desire women who laugh at their jokes, whereas women prefer men who can make them laugh."[14] After a relationship is established, the role of laughter changes, but it's no less important. For example, women in committed relationships value laughter and humor for their ability to "relieve tense discussions."[15]

In chapter 2 we listed many of the health benefits associated with laughter. Consider these important benefits:

- Laughter contributes to normal blood flow. The University of Maryland conducted a study in which some subjects watched a funny movie while others watched a drama. Afterward, those who had watched the comedy demonstrated normal blood flow in their vessels, while those who had watched the drama had tensed up, restricting blood flow.[16]

- Laughter boosts your immunity. Studies show that laughter may boost the body's ability to fight infection.[17]
- Laughter contributes to better relaxation and satisfying sleep.[18]

You probably know from experience that laughter can help improve relationships as well. Think of some of your favorite times with family and friends. Chances are, many of those memories involve moments of fun and laughter. The ability to laugh together helps us bond with one another!

Activity: Create an opportunity to laugh together. The success of this date depends on your knowing each other well enough to understand what your partner finds funny. It could be something as simple as sitting across the table from each other and telling funny stories. Or it could involve something more adventurous, such as going to a comedy club or a funny movie. (Yes, we remember suggesting earlier in the book that you not make moviegoing a regular dating activity. But you can make exceptions once in a while. In this case, just be sure the movie is something that will elicit laughter from both of you, and be sure to save time afterward to talk about it and laugh some more.) You might also consider visiting a bookstore or going online and finding a book of clean jokes or Mad Libs.

Questions: Ask each other these questions: What makes you laugh? What about our activity did you find particularly funny? Also talk about the art of laughing at yourself. Are there some silly or funny quirks about your spouse that you find irresistibly funny? Maybe her set of 1950s-vintage hair curlers, or his Snoopy boxer shorts? Be sure to pick things that are lighthearted and fun. Don't laugh at your spouse's expense or be cruel.

They're Just Like Two Kids in Love . . .

We don't stop playing because we grow old;
we grow old because we stop playing.
—George Bernard Shaw

When was the last time you felt like you played? For most of us, play-time is a vestige of childhood. We left it behind when we entered the world of adulthood. Respectable folks who are raising kids, holding down jobs, serving at church, and making meaningful contributions to society don't play, do they? After all, the apostle Paul himself said, "When I was a child, I talked like a child, I thought like a child, I reasoned like a child. When I became a man, I put childish ways behind me" (1 Corinthians 13:11). Hrrumph!

We certainly don't question the authority of Paul's words, which are the inspired Word of God. But if that verse hangs over your head as an admonition against having fun or taking time to play and recreate, then we'd suggest that 1 Corinthians 13:11 doesn't mean quite what you think it means.

Now certainly, if you're spending several hours every day playing your Xbox 360, you're playing too much. Lord knows, countless men today, both inside and outside the church, seem to be stuck in a period of extended adolescence. They really *do* play video games for hours at a time and engage in all sorts of other activities that may not be inappropriate on the surface but, when taken to extremes, are a genuine affront to the concepts of responsibility and maturity. Women aren't immune to this problem either.

Within reason, however, there's nothing wrong with responsible, upstanding adults having fun and engaging in leisure activities from time to time. These pursuits are actually essential to your emotional and mental health. And there's certainly a case to be made for husbands and wives enjoying playtime *together* on occasion. That's what this date is all about.

Activity: You can both probably name some things you like to do when it comes to leisure activities. You're certainly free to select something from your current list of favorites that you'd both find enjoyable. But to make things more interesting, why not consider something you haven't done for a while—maybe for a *long* while? Maybe not even since you were kids? Talk about some of your favorite *childhood* playtime activities and then consider incorporating one or more of them into your date. Here are some examples:

- Go to a ball game. Make sure to eat lots of peanuts and ice cream.
- Go to an amusement park. Load up on hot dogs and cotton candy—but ride the roller coaster *first*!
- Find an old board game or even a set of marbles and play a few rounds together.
- Have a tea party complete with fancy cups and saucers. Instead of serving tea to your dollies, serve each other.

Questions: This date presents a great opportunity to dig a little deeper into any preconceptions you may have about leisure time. Discuss the following questions: Do you have happy childhood memories? What were some of your favorite things to play as a child? How did your family view playtime? Was it frowned upon or encouraged?

Read Ecclesiastes chapter 3 together ("There is a time for everything, and a season for every activity under heaven . . ." [verse 1]). Then discuss these questions: Do you think leisure time fits into this passage somewhere? How can we be more intentional about including reasonable amounts of playtime in our schedule?

Sweat

I like to move it, move it. She likes to
move it, move it. He likes to move it,
move it. You like to—move it!
—"I Like to Move It," from *Madagascar*

In 2011 the Bureau of Labor Statistics found that the amount of time people (fifteen years of age and older) engaged in a sports or exercise activity on an average day in the United States was eighteen minutes. But the time people spent watching TV on an average day was almost *ten times* that amount![19]

While it's certainly true that many Americans seem to have an aversion to physical activity and eschew it altogether, others carry exercise to the opposite extreme. A study in the *Mayo Clinic Proceedings*, for example, found that while people who exercise regularly enjoy tremendous health benefits, those who train hard for triathlons, ultramarathons, and other extreme events have a much greater risk of suffering serious heart damage.[20]

There has to be a happy medium somewhere, right? Its somewhere between having a heart attack because you're a couch potato and having a heart attack because you're an extreme-sports junkie. Hopefully you and your spouse share a commitment to regular physical exercise, whether it means a workout program at the gym, walks or jogs around the neighborhood, or even just good old-fashioned outdoor work in the form of landscaping, yard work, and so on. You know, the kind of work, like farming, that people used to do just to survive, before gyms were invented.

If you're like most American families, you probably don't exercise together very often. Due to the demands of work, parenting, and other activities, it simply isn't practical to do so. However, since you'll be setting aside some couple time for a date anyway, why not consider making exercise a shared activity?

Activity: If you typically go to a gym to work out, take your spouse along this time. (Some gyms, such as Curves, are women-only establishments, so be sensitive to any rules and restrictions.) Teach your spouse your workout routine. If time and circumstances allow, do something more ambitious. Try something you haven't done before, such as rock climbing or kayaking. If you'd like to engage in something more long term together, consider training for a half marathon or registering for a local charity run.

Bonus activity: Many people use fast-paced music to exercise. When you have some free time, create a workout "playlist" together that includes some of your and your spouse's favorite workout songs. Then make sure the playlist is available on both of your devices. This is a great way to be reminded of your spouse the next time you're working out on your own. Plus, you just might discover some new tunes to get your heart rate moving. Your wife might learn to kick it old skool with "Eye of the Tiger" by Survivor, while your husband might have his musical horizons expanded by being introduced to the foot-stompin' vibes of "I Gotta Feeling" by the Black Eyed Peas.

Questions: After your activity (and perhaps a shower and a bottle of Gatorade!), discuss the following questions: How important is physical fitness to you? How can we encourage each other (and our kids) in the pursuit of a balanced approach to physical fitness—not too lax and not too extreme? During our physical activity, what was one thing you learned about me that you didn't know before?

Looking Forward

Life can only be understood backwards;
but it must be lived forwards.
—Søren Kierkegaard

What will your marriage look like one year from now? How about two years? Ten years? At the beginning of this chapter, you enjoyed a New Year's date, during which you looked ahead to the coming year and set goals for your relationship and your marriage. Now it's time to take that same concept and cast a longer-term vision for the future.

This process isn't about making concrete plans or administrating the next decade of your relationship. Carrying this concept too far will only lead to frustration, and besides, it's not biblical. The apostle James reminds us,

> Now listen, you who say, "Today or tomorrow we will go to
> this or that city, spend a year there, carry on business and make
> money." Why, you do not even know what will happen tomor-
> row. What is your life? You are a mist that appears for a little
> while and then vanishes. (James 4:13–14)

It's true. If the Lord tarries, the years ahead in your marriage will bring many unexpected blessings, and many unexpected trials. They will be filled with events and occurrences for which you simply couldn't have planned. That's part of the deal. It's also one of the reasons you made a commitment on your wedding day to love each other "for better or for worse." You simply don't know what forms the better and the worse will take until they reveal themselves in the course of God's good timing.

What you *can* do, though, is set goals for your relationship that will help you grow closer and more intimate throughout the remaining years of your marriage, through the good and bad times that are sure to come. Together you can embrace God's awesome promise: "I know the plans I have for you . . . plans to prosper you and not to harm you, plans to give you hope and a future" (Jeremiah 29:11).

Activity: For your New Year's date, we recommended that you engage in a morning activity, such as going out for breakfast or taking an invigorating hike. We'd like to suggest a morning activity for this date as well. In our experience, thinking, praying, and casting a vision for the future are easier to do under sunny skies at the start of a new day than they are in the dark of night. So get up, go outdoors, and breathe in the possibilities!

Questions: After your activity, sit down and talk about your future together. Don't get bogged down in the details of career, childrearing, and so forth. Rather, focus on the aspects of your married relationship that you want to enhance in the coming years. How do we envision our future together? What aspects of our relationship do we want to enhance together on the road ahead? You might even consider writing a marriage mission statement together. Talk about your shared vision and values for your relationship, and then craft a brief, simple statement together that encapsulates those values. For example, "We will pursue intimacy with God and with each other for the sake of our children, the world around us, and the glory of God." (*Note*: Some couples write marriage mission statements during the course of their premarital counseling. If you did this, see if you can dig it out, and then evaluate how you're doing. Are you meeting the goals you put on paper during your engagement? What, if anything, would you change or revise about the statement now that you have x years of marriage under your belts?)

Sprucing Up the Nest

The sun at home warms better
than the sun elsewhere.
—Albanian proverb

You probably have special memories from childhood that are tied directly to your surroundings at the time. For example, you may see a wallpaper design now that reminds you of the quilt you had on your bed when you were little. Or maybe you've created a special space in your home now—even if it's just a corner of a room or a desktop or some other nook or cranny—that reminds you of a similarly special space, a place of refuge, that you enjoyed at home as a child.

There's something comforting about having so many wonderful memories contained within the four actual walls of your home. And even if you didn't have those special memories growing up, it's a blessing to be able to invest in them and create them now—for your marriage and your kids. This date will give you the opportunity to invest some time and energy in making your home beautiful, whatever that might mean to you.

Men, you may be rolling your eyes right now. "I can't believe it! My wife has been pestering me for months to paint the family room, and now Greg and Erin have the audacity to suggest that we actually turn that dreadful chore into a *date*. No way!"

Before you run for the hills, hear us out! One of the points we've been trying to make throughout this book is that in addition to carving out time for dating, husbands and wives have the opportunity to build intimacy through their *everyday activities*. It's true, doing household chores doesn't automatically bring to mind romance. But there's no reason these activities have to be routine and mundane. They're only mindless chores if you allow them to be. So pick something around the house that needs doing, and *do it*! But do it together, and make it fun.

Here's an example from our own experience: One time when we were folding laundry together, Erin went up to get some more dirty clothes from the kids' rooms. While she was upstairs, the washing machine finished, and I (Greg) went to unload it. I noticed our five-year-old daughter standing next to me, begging to help. A devilish plan formed in my mind. I talked my daughter into hiding in the empty dryer without really considering the consequences or realizing the danger. I then waited for Erin. When she returned, she dropped the dirty clothes into the laundry basket and took the clean load out of the washing machine. I silently peeked around the corner and watched her move toward the dryer. When Erin opened the door to throw in the wet clothes, our daughter screamed and grabbed her arm. It was awesome! Erin jumped about four feet in the air and ran out of the laundry room screaming. I'll spare you the ugly details—let's just say that I ended up doing the rest of the laundry by myself. But you know what? It turned a mundane chore into something fun that we still laugh about today—even Erin.

Activity: Paint a room, put up wallpaper, install carpet, clean out the basement—anything that will spruce up your house. Have fun investing in the beauty of your home, making it a fun and inviting space that lends itself to building happy memories. Turn what could be a mundane chore or a looming responsibility into a fun chance to connect.

And here's something that will definitely make the process more interesting (and appealing): At the end of your project, you'll likely be dirty. You may have paint all over your face or grime in your hair, or you may just be good and sweaty. Why don't you resolve to help each other clean up after your project is finished (and after the kids are in bed)? Perhaps you can take a hot bath or shower together to help scrub all those hard-to-reach places on your partner. Then you can head to bed to massage all the sore muscles your spouse developed during the project. Who knows what other activities might come to mind as you endeavor to unwind from your house beautifying project!

See? Suddenly repainting the family room doesn't seem like such a bad idea, does it, guys? All you need is to figure out some creative ways to end on a high note!

Questions: As you work on your home-improvement project, share memories of your childhoods and the roles that your living spaces played in those memories. Ask each other these questions: What specific rooms, pieces of furniture, colors, or designs made an impression on you in your childhood home? What special memories do you have of your living space as a child? How important is our home environment now to creating good memories for us and our children?

Listen Up!

My wife says I never listen to her.
At least I think that's what she said.
—Author unknown

Communication is a key ingredient in any healthy marriage. And one of the most important components of good communication is *listening*. The Bible reminds us that we are to be "quick to listen, slow to speak and slow to become angry" (James 1:19).

The simple act of listening—of actually hearing and absorbing what your spouse is saying—conveys several important messages. It signifies that you want to *understand* your spouse not just in terms of the words being used but in terms of the feelings behind those words. Listening also helps you *validate* your spouse. As a rule, your mate will desire to communicate with you only to the degree that he or she feels heard and understood. Finally, listening helps you develop *empathy* for your spouse. Empathy goes beyond "I understand what you're feeling" and says, "I feel what you're feeling."

Activity: You may be tempted to say, "Uh-oh, Greg and Erin. We're talking about communication and empathy now. That sounds very, um, 'diagnostic.' Are we going to break the rules you set forth and start administrating our dates?"

Don't worry, we're not going to get all "marriage counselor" on you. For this date, pick a fun activity that you both enjoy, such as going out for a nice dinner, bowling, to a coffee shop, or to the ballet. Or go see a movie or a play that you can discuss afterward—you know, so that you can put those *communication* skills to work! As always, have *fun*!

Questions: Even within the context of a fun date, there's no reason why you can't talk about your marital communication skills in an uplifting, positive manner. After your activity, talk about ways you can communicate more effectively. This isn't a time to berate or criticize your spouse; it's simply an opportunity to invest in healthy communication, which will in turn deepen your intimacy. Ask yourselves, "What are some ways we can more effectively incorporate understanding, validation, and empathy into our communication as a couple?"

Rest

God made time, but man made haste.
—Irish proverb

We've already mentioned, at several points in this book, the problems posed by our frantic twenty-first-century lifestyle. Being busy all day every day robs us of quality time with our families. It erects a barrier to important couple time and intimacy. Rushing headlong from one commitment to the next creates stress, which can become overwhelming and even debilitating. In fact, WebMD reports that stress contributes to headaches, high blood pressure, heart problems, diabetes, asthma, and depression, among other problems. In fact, studies show that "stress-related ailments and complaints" comprise between 75 and 90 percent of all doctor's office visits![21]

You also need to know that if you're living at a frantic pace, you're potentially doing damage to your kids as well. How's that for a guilt trip? A Finnish study found that the children of parents who suffer from burnout are more likely to suffer from burnout themselves.[22] This is really just common sense. We already know that we have the greatest influence on our kids by what we *show* them rather than what we *tell* them. Hopefully those two aspects of our parenting will reinforce each other, but often that isn't the case. If we "preach" at our kids about getting adequate rest and taking time to refresh, all while we're living chaotic, eighteen-hour days and literally fighting to keep control of the ship, what can we really expect? Of course our kids are going to model our destructive behavior!

For the sake of our marriages, and our kids, we must create space in our lives for a little downtime. We would do well to heed the words of David: "I have stilled and quieted my soul; like a weaned child with its mother, like a weaned child is my soul within me" (Psalm 131:2).

Activity: Here's your chance to do something spontaneous and relaxing. Whatever you do, make sure you allow plenty of time beforehand so you're not *rushing* to your destination. You're defeating the purpose if you have to hurry up and relax! The activity itself will depend on what the two of you find especially soothing, but here are a few ideas:

- Get a couples' massage (from a reputable therapist, of course—don't rely on dodgy ads in the back of your local alternative newspaper!).

- Many Middle Eastern restaurants serve patrons in the traditional style—i.e., sitting on the floor and reclining on pillows, and so on. See if you can find a Moroccan, Afghan, or similar restaurant that offers this relaxing feature. Some Japanese restaurants serve in this style as well. It's a very low-key, soothing way to dine. Hey, if it was good enough for Jesus and the disciples . . .

- Stay home and enjoy the feeling of not having to go anywhere! Enjoy a hot bath together or some time in the hot tub. Put on some relaxing music. Cuddle in front of the fireplace.

Questions: As you relax and unwind together, discuss the following questions: How can we create "margin" in our lives? (Dr. Richard Swenson defines *margin* as "the space between our load and our limits. It is the amount allowed beyond that which is needed. . . . It is something held in reserve for contingencies or unanticipated situations. Margin is the gap between rest and exhaustion, the space between breathing freely and suffocating."[23]) Are there unnecessary commitments we can cut out of our schedules for the sake of our family's health and vitality? How can we model healthy limits to each other and to our kids?

Encourage

There are two ways of exerting one's strength:
one is pushing down, the other is pulling up.
—Booker T. Washington

The word *encourage* literally means "to make courageous." It's more than saying something nice about people. It's lifting them up and affirming them to the point that they say, "I can do this!" in the face of something that might otherwise seem too challenging, too frightening, or too difficult.

That's a wonderful picture of what happens in marriage, isn't it? Throughout the course of your relationship, you'll face many struggles, whether unemployment, illness, disease, bankruptcy, childrearing challenges, or just everyday hurts and disappointments. There will be many good times, too, of course. The point is that in marriage, the hills and valleys are easier to take when you have someone in your corner. Out-of-control kids and overwhelming credit-card bills can either tear you apart or pull you closer together. It all depends on your ability to tackle these challenges with a united front. Husbands and wives can *encourage* each other—literally make each other courageous—in the face of life's ups and downs.

One of our favorite "excuses" to go on a date is after a bad day. Several months ago, I (Greg) was taking our son to school during a brutal snowstorm. We'd all been hoping for a snow day, but no dice. I managed to navigate the treacherous roads and drop him off at school, but I was running late and needed to be at work for an important meeting. I was following a minivan out of the school parking lot when I realized that my seat belt wasn't buckled. I looked down for a mere second to buckle up, and—you guessed it—*CRASH*! I watched as the minivan's rear light and bumper fell to the ground.

The woman I hit was very understanding, and because of the nor'easter taking place, I asked her if we could sit inside my car while I called the insurance company. I handed the woman my license so she could write down my information. As she was recording my name, a very familiar commercial started to play on the radio. It was for an upcoming father-daughter banquet and dance. This has been a popular event in Colorado Springs for the past fifteen years. Thousands of fathers and daughters get dressed up for an unbelievable date night together.

"Hey," the lady said as she continued to write, "my husband and daughter are going to that!"

And then the part of the commercial came that I was dreading: "featuring special guest speaker Dr. Greg Smalley." I smiled as the woman looked at the radio, looked at my driver's license, and then looked at me. "Yes,"—I nodded, embarrassed—"I'm the speaker. I can't drive, but I can speak!"

Later that day, Erin roared with laughter as I recounted my terrible morning. "Only you would hit someone who'll be at one of your speaking engagements!" But then she said something that instantly lifted my spirits. "Why don't you and I go on a date tonight? We could both use a fun evening." She had only one condition: I had to let her drive!

Another way to encourage your spouse on a date is to help him or her try something new. Have you ever wanted to try something but were too nervous or afraid? Perhaps the activity itself appeals to you, but you've never taken the plunge because you lack confidence. You may feel you just don't have what it takes. It could be a demanding physical activity or something like public speaking or even dancing. If you're willing to be a little adventurous, this date will allow you to indulge that desire as a team, encouraging each other along the way.

Activity: If time and budget allow, don't be afraid to go for the gusto here. Try something challenging! Don't put yourselves in any danger, of course, but try to find an activity that lies outside your normal comfort zone. And as you did with the teamwork date earlier, focus on completing it together, offering lots of encouragement and affirmation to your partner along the way. Here are some possible activities:

- Singing karaoke
- Participating in a poetry night at a local venue
- Riding the scariest, most heart-attack-inducing roller coaster you can find

Questions: After your activity, bring the principles of encouragement back to the real world. You might not jump out of an airplane every day, but you *will* face challenging situations, whether dealing with unruly kids, giving an important presentation at work, or managing hostile employees or coworkers. Ask your spouse, "How can I encourage you as you face upcoming challenges?" "What do you dread during the week that I can help you face?"

Traditions

What an enormous magnifier is tradition!
How a thing grows in the human memory
and in the human imagination,
when love, worship, and all that lies in the
human heart, is there to encourage it.
—Thomas Carlyle

Traditions are among the bedrocks of family life. Countless books have been written, from both Christian and non-Christian perspectives, on how to build traditions in the home. Many of these are centered around the holidays, birthdays, and other special occasions. When you read the title of this date, it's likely that a few of your own family traditions immediately popped into your head. Attending the midnight service on Christmas Eve, spending a midsummer weekend at the lake, going on a father-son hunting trip in the fall. Whatever they are, your family likely has a handful of special traditions that you hold dear.

But what about traditions related specifically to your marriage? Are there any special customs you and your spouse share and treasure? We're not talking about yearly observances like your anniversary or birthdays (although those are important). We're talking about unique events that are important only to the two of you—things that other folks don't necessarily understand. Maybe it's having a weekend getaway, just the two of you, at a favorite nearby destination. Or perhaps it's something as simple as going out for coffee on the first Saturday morning of every month. Whatever the details, maintaining special husband-wife traditions is a great way to build intimacy.

Activity: If you have a cherished couples-only tradition you enjoy, center your date around it! Go out for a nice dinner and plan your next weekend at the mountain chalet. Do you put a complex puzzle together every New Year's Eve? Go to the store now, a few months early, and pick out the puzzle. If you don't have any special traditions as a couple, why not use this opportunity to start one? The possibilities are limited only by your imagination.

Questions: As you engage in your activity, discuss the following questions: Did you have special traditions in your family growing up? What were they? What do you remember most about them? How can we create and maintain traditions for our marriage? For our family?

Time for a Checkup!

*There is no more lovely, friendly
and charming relationship, communion
or company than a good marriage.*
—Martin Luther

Okay, we've already said many times throughout this book that your dates should be characterized by fun; they are *not* for administrating your marriage or addressing problems and conflicts. A couple of the dates thus far have skirted close to administration territory without actually crossing over.

This date will be slightly different. It involves both spouses taking an online assessment known as Focus on the Family's "Couple Checkup." Each of you will go to the website *focusonthefamily.com/couplecheckup* and answer roughly 120 questions related to communication, roles, finances, affection, conflict, and other aspects of married life. (There's a one-time $29.95 charge for the checkup, and there are versions for dating, engaged, and married couples.)

The "Couple Checkup" is backed by more than twenty years of research. Focus on the Family's version has been customized to reflect a distinctly Christian, or biblical, view of marriage. After each of you completes the assessment, you'll have a well-rounded overview of your relationship that will give you insight not only into growth areas but also into your strengths as a couple.

Is taking the "Couple Checkup" the same thing as administrating your marriage? To be honest, yes. There's no point in suggesting otherwise. However, that doesn't mean it has to put a damper on your date-night fun. Think of it as a tool you can use to make your marriage even stronger—to deepen your intimacy with and commitment to each other. Taking the assessment doesn't necessarily suggest that your marriage is in trouble and needs help. Rather, it's a proactive step you can take that signifies a commitment on both of your parts to make your marriage the best it can be.

Activity: Prior to your date, each of you should visit *focuson thefamily.com/couplecheckup* and take the assessment individually. It typically takes around thirty minutes to complete. Once you've both finished the checkup, print out your results and take them with you on your date. The activity itself can be a nice dinner, a visit to a museum, a walk around the lake, or another activity you both enjoy.

Questions: After your activity is over, go to a quiet location where you can have a hot cup of coffee or another beverage, and pull out your assessments. Discuss the results together. Pay attention to those areas in which you're thriving as a couple, as well as those areas that could use some work. Don't be discouraged by any growth areas. Talk about them together and be positive and affirming about ways you can help your relationship grow. Going through the entire assessment may be too much for one date, so commit to completing the process at home or on your next date.

If the process of going through the "Couple Checkup" seems too daunting to accomplish on your own, you might consider getting in touch with another couple you respect, or a pastor, mentor, or even a professional counselor if you believe you need extra help. You can contact Focus on the Family at 1-800-A-FAMILY or *focusonthe family.com* for assistance in locating a counselor in your area.

The Weekend Getaway

Come away with me, and we'll kiss
on a mountaintop; come away with
me and I'll never stop loving you.
—Norah Jones, "Come Away with Me"

The weekend getaway takes all of the dating principles we've been discussing thus far and expands them into a full-blown, multiday event! A regular date night allows you to break free from the common challenges and distractions of home (kids, homework, household chores, etc.) for a few hours of uninterrupted couple time. A weekend getaway does the same thing but allows considerably more precious time for you and your spouse to relax, have fun, and connect. Sometimes you need more than just a few hours once a week or once a month. In fact, some marriage experts recommend that husbands and wives schedule at least one or two weekends away *every year*.

Of course, the same challenges to regular date nights (budget concerns, a packed calendar, childcare needs, etc.) are exacerbated when it comes to putting together a weekend getaway. However, with some creativity and determination, we believe that most of these obstacles can be overcome. For example, when it comes to your budget, research some modestly priced motels, bed-and-breakfasts, or even a friend's time-share or vacation home within driving distance. There's no need to fly to a faraway destination or stay at a luxurious resort. When it comes to childcare, call upon friends, relatives, or other trusted families in your church. In chapter 2 we explained the benefits of a babysitting co-op in which couples trade childcare responsibilities throughout the month so their peers can go on dates. The same principle applies here. Find a family who is willing and able to watch your kids for the entire weekend—and make sure you're willing to do the same for them when the need arises!

Activity: Since you'll be away for one or two nights, as well as the better part of two days, you'll have time for plenty of activities. But don't succumb to the temptation to fill every available moment with planned events! Sometimes it's best just to get away, relax, and enjoy unstructured downtime. Sleep late. Pray together. Take long walks. Make love. Talk about your hopes and dreams. If you feel up to it, visit some local attractions. Whatever you do, *don't let work intrude on your weekend*! Smartphones, iPads, and other devices should be reserved for occasional contact with your children and their caretakers *only*. Checking email and Facebook is strictly forbidden! As with your regular date night, the weekend getaway is about having fun, investing in each other, and fostering intimacy. Don't administrate your marriage and don't spend a lot of time talking about heavy or contentious issues.

Questions: If you recently completed Focus on the Family's "Couple Checkup" (see previous date), a weekend getaway would be a great opportunity to talk about some of the things you learned about yourself and your spouse. Don't feel pressure to troubleshoot or solve any perceived problems that you may have discerned after taking the checkup. Rather, accentuate the positive and talk about areas in which you feel you're excelling. Also look back over some of the discussion questions from your previous date nights and see if they lend themselves to deeper conversations than what would have been possible on a standard date night.

Vive La Différence!

It were not best that we should all think alike;
it is difference of opinion that makes horse races.
—Mark Twain, *Pudd'nhead Wilson's Calendar*

Earlier in the chapter we outlined a date designed to help you and
your spouse find common interests—hobbies or activities that you
both enjoy. That's all well and good, but having areas of shared interest
doesn't mean you have to abandon those things that are uniquely you.
Guys, you might enjoy watching football, but no matter how much
you might wish otherwise, that activity may never appeal to your
wives. And ladies, you may find scrapbooking to be an invigorating
and fulfilling pursuit, but your husbands may never "get it." (Lest you
think we're being sexist here, we're sure that plenty of women out there
love watching football and plenty of men relish scrapbooking. Hey,
it could happen!) Here's just a brief smattering of some of our own
diverse interests. Erin enjoys these activities:

- Bargain shopping
- Going on walks with friends
- Working out
- Bible study
- Watching the series Downton Abbey and romantic comedies
- Enjoying mocha lattes
- Working in her flower garden
- Cooking

Greg, on the other hand, enjoys the following:

- Watching football and other sports
- Playing video games with the kids
- Skiing
- Fishing
- Working out on the treadmill
- Watching action movies
- Eating!

The point is, it's okay to have interests and passions that are unique to *you*, even if your spouse doesn't share them. Husbands and wives who allow themselves to like and dislike only the same things their spouses do can end up looking like clones of each other. It can diminish their unique, God-given personalities. It can also lead to resentment. Husbands who embrace their wives' hobbies or wives who embrace their husbands' hobbies—not because they find them interesting but because they're expected to do so to keep the peace—will likely end up harboring bitterness. Deep down they may feel as if their spouse doesn't understand them or respect them.

So go ahead and embrace your differences! For this date, you'll pick out two activities—one that appeals uniquely to the husband, and one that appeals uniquely to the wife. If time won't allow for you to engage in both activities during the course of one date, feel free to make two dates out of it.

Activity: Here's the deal, though. The purpose of this date isn't to flaunt something you enjoy while your partner is miserable. Nor is the idea to force your spouse into doing something in the hope that he or she will, finally, see the light and enjoy it. Rather, it's to do something you're passionate about to give your spouse a deeper insight into your interests, your personality, and the things that drive you. So pick something you truly enjoy—and let your spouse do the same, either on this date or the next—and then be prepared to discuss and answer questions about why this activity is so important to you, and why you enjoy it so much.

Here are a few things guys might find fun and a few things gals might find fun. But don't feel constrained by these lists, and don't feel bad if something you enjoy appears on the opposite gender list. These are just suggestions to get you thinking about the things you uniquely enjoy:

Men	*Women*
Attend a college or pro sports event	Go to a restaurant with exotic cuisine
Attend a monster truck rally	Go shopping together
Play paintball	Watch a romantic movie together
Attend a rock concert	Attend a ballet production

Find something that highlights the differences in your personalities, preferences, or even gender. Unlike shared interests, you don't have to embrace your spouse's chosen pursuit, but you can appreciate it for what it tells you about your spouse.

Questions: Whatever activities you chose, remember, the point wasn't to make one spouse suffer through something only the other spouse loves. Rather, it was to help you gain an appreciation for your mate's unique interests and passions. For example, as a woman, you may not relish playing paintball, but did it help you appreciate your husband's go-get-'em attitude? As a man, you may loathe shopping, but did shopping with your wife give you a greater admiration for her frugality or her sense of style?

After your activities are over, discuss the following questions: Did you find it challenging to engage in my chosen activity? How did it make you feel? Does experiencing it make you appreciate me more?

Stolen Moments

Summer's going fast, nights growing colder;
children growing up, old friends growing older.
Freeze this moment a little bit longer,
make each sensation a little bit stronger.
—Rush, "Time Stand Still"

The alarm buzzes and the day begins. You jump out of bed and hit the ground running. You have just enough time to say a quick prayer and read a Bible verse before hitting the shower, getting dressed, and scrambling to the kitchen for breakfast—or maybe just some coffee to drink in the car. But don't forget the kids! They also need to dress, eat, and get ready for the day—and it's up to you to help make it all happen.

Sound familiar? Most families run through this routine, or something similar, every morning. Your blood pressure is probably rising just thinking about it. And the end of the day isn't any different. It's a mad dash from school to extracurricular activities and then maybe the grocery store and some other errands. Then it's home for dinner, the kids' homework, and numerous household responsibilities before you finally fall into bed, exhausted.

You can't avoid these everyday responsibilities, but what if, for the sake of your marriage, you started to view them as *opportunities* rather than just the day-to-day grind? Is it possible for you and your spouse to experience emotional and relational *connection* in the midst of a busy day? The answer is a resounding *yes*!

Waking up in the morning, getting yourself and your kids ready, having devotional time, eating breakfast, and maybe working out—all of these are opportunities for you and your spouse to connect and start the day right. They present the chance for husbands and wives to compliment and encourage each other—to work *together*. By the time everyone leaves the house, you can either be frazzled and cranky with one another or feel you've made a genuine, intimate connection amid the hustle and bustle. Whether in the morning or the evening, or even during the day when you're apart, you just need to have a plan for maximizing those everyday moments.

Activity: You know the drill! Do something *fun*, and if possible, something you haven't tried before. Go to a Nepalese restaurant. Visit the local wax museum. Try country swing dancing.

Questions: After your activity, go to a coffee shop or someplace quiet and talk about ways to maximize everyday moments. Have fun exploring ways you can foster intimacy with each other, even amid the chaos of everyday life.

For example, in the *morning*, you might enjoy these activities:

- Take a few moments to cuddle and affirm your love for each other before getting out of bed.
- Prepare breakfast *together*.
- Get the kids ready *together*.
- Read a passage of Scripture and/or pray over the day *together*.
- If your kids are old enough to be left alone, go on a quick jog around the block *together*. (Just make sure your kids are aware of this plan the night before!)
- Compliment and affirm each other as you prepare for the day.
- Actually kiss good-bye before heading out the door!

At *midday*, when you're typically apart, you might do the following:

- Send quick texts or emails to say, "I love you and I'm thinking about you."
- Make phone calls to check in. (Even if you know your spouse is in a meeting or otherwise unavailable, call and leave a romantic voice mail!)
- Send an occasional bouquet or other surprise delivery. Don't save this idea just for anniversaries and other special occasions!
- Meet at a restaurant for a lunch date.
- If time and your schedules allow, meet back at home for a quick romantic interlude!

In the *evening*, you could reconnect in any of these ways:

- Without fail, stop what you're doing and greet your spouse with a kiss when he or she walks through the door.
- Make dinner together.
- Get the kids ready for bed together.
- Enjoy some downtime together—watch a favorite TV show, read and discuss a book, play a board game, or do something else you both enjoy.
- At bedtime, share words of affirmation and praise for your spouse. Be specific!
- Pray together.
- Before rolling over and going to sleep, be sure to kiss good night—like you mean it!

Touch

Hands, touchin' hands; reachin' out,
touchin' me, touchin' you.
—Neil Diamond, "Sweet Caroline"

In date 5 ("The Blessing") we outlined a date focused on the five elements of blessing our spouses. You probably recall that one of the ways we communicate blessing to our spouses (as well as to our children) is through *meaningful touch*. In the context of marriage, sexual touch is certainly part of the equation, but meaningful touch for couples takes many other forms as well. It may be the way a husband puts his hand on the small of his wife's back as they navigate a crowded room together, or the way a wife places her hand on her husband's knee as they're driving around town. Holding hands while walking around town, putting an arm around your mate's shoulders while sitting in the pew in church, cradling your beloved's face in your hands while you kiss, patting your spouse on the back in an effort to encourage him or her—all of these expressions communicate love, intimacy, and acceptance.

Studies show that people who are comfortable with touch in relationships are more "talkative" and "cheerful," while those uncomfortable with touching tend to be more "emotionally unstable and socially withdrawn."[24] It's also worth noting that physical touch is one of the five "love languages" identified by Dr. Gary Chapman as ways to express love emotionally. (The other four love languages are words of affirmation, quality time, receiving gifts, and acts of service.)[25] If physical touch is your spouse's primary love language, then it's especially important that you become an expert in expressing love in this way!

Activity: Pick a typical activity, or get creative and come up with something that involves the sense of touch. Take a nature hike and experience the contrast in texture between tree bark, flower petals, and cold, hard stones (just avoid the poison ivy!). Or visit a fabric store and consider the differences between wool, silk, and other fabrics.

Questions: After your activity, go someplace quiet for coffee and dessert and discuss how the art of touch can communicate intimacy in your marriage. Is meaningful touch your primary love language? How do you feel when I put my arm around you in church or reach out for your hand when we're walking? What kind of touch do you respond to? What are some other ways we can incorporate meaningful touch into our daily routine?

When you get home, don't hesitate to cap off your date with more touching—sexual or nonsexual. Give each other a back rub, run your fingers through each other's hair, and so on!

Simple Gifts

A wise lover values not so much the gift of Him
Who loves as the love of Him Who gives.
—Thomas à Kempis, *The Imitation of Christ*

Giving gifts to your spouse can be a fun way to build intimacy—
if they're given in the right spirit and for the right reasons! We've
all heard about (usually older) men who lavish their (usually much
younger) wives with diamonds, cars, vacations, and the latest fashions
from Milan, Italy, on a regular basis. In many cases, there is no true intimacy in the relationship; one spouse is simply endeavoring to "buy"
the affection of the other. Bombarding your spouse with piles of stuff
to prove your love or to show other people how awesome you are isn't
a shortcut to intimacy.

But gifts invested with love, affection, and thought convey a different message. They're a simple way to let your spouse know you value
and appreciate him or her. The gift doesn't have to be extravagant or
expensive. It could even be homemade. The important thing is that it
conveys a meaningful message about your feelings for your spouse or
communicates something particular about your relationship.

Sometimes the item itself might be a flop. Have you ever mentioned needing a new pair of winter gloves or a new golf putter only
to have your spouse surprise you a couple of days later with the new
item? The gloves might end up being too big or the wrong color, and
the putter might not match the rest of your golf clubs. But at that
point it doesn't matter. The message that has been conveyed is that

your spouse listens to you and cares about the things you care about. What do you usually say when you receive a gift like this? "It's the thought that counts." And that's absolutely true.

Activity: Go shopping, preferably at the mall or a large department store. Then split up! Each of you should try to purchase something your spouse would find meaningful; something that reminds you of him or her. Again, don't feel the need to spend a lot of money. The item could be something as simple as a new neon cell-phone case for your wife to replace the one that broke, or a new ball cap featuring the logo of your husband's favorite team (okay, sometimes those do get a bit pricey). The idea is to find something that lets your spouse know you're in tune with his or her interests and needs. After you've had a chance to find a gift, meet up again at a predetermined time for a gift exchange.

Alternatively, if you have time in the days leading up to your date, why not try to make a gift for your spouse? It doesn't need to be complicated—perhaps putting together a simple scrapbook page of photos of the two of you having fun together, or even creating a playlist of some of your spouse's favorite songs and putting them on his or her iPod.

Questions: After you've exchanged gifts, discuss the following questions: Why did you pick this gift? What about it made you think of me? How important are simple gifts like this to you in terms of communicating intimacy? Do you have any favorite gifts or mementos from early in our marriage that you still cherish?

Double-Date!

*Friendship is not a reward for our
discrimination and good taste in finding one
another out. It is the instrument by which God
reveals to each the beauties of all the others.*
—C. S. Lewis, *The Four Loves*

Here's another instance in which you'll deviate slightly from the standard date-night format. In general we recommend that your dates be
devoted to couple time (i.e., uninterrupted time between just the two
of you, without the distractions of kids or other adults). *However,*
once in a while, it's a good idea to venture outside of that format
and enjoy a date with another couple. In fact, later in this book we'll
devote an entire chapter to the benefits of building relationships with
other couples.

For the purposes of this discussion, we'll assume that you'll be
dating with a "peer" couple—a couple who is in generally the same
stage of life you're in and who is roughly the same age. In chapter 6
we'll address double dating in greater depth, as well as discuss the
possibilities afforded by going on double dates with couples who are
younger than you are (recently married and likely still without kids),
couples who are older than you (whose kids are nearly grown or no
longer living at home), and couples whom you've only recently met
(those whom you wouldn't yet consider close friends or confidants).

But for now, let's stick with a couple you know and trust. The most likely candidate would be a couple from church or longtime friends, or perhaps another couple from your babysitting co-op.

Just as on your regular dates, avoid the temptation to administrate during your double date. For most couples during the childrearing years, the standard procedure is to go out together and tell story after story about the *kids*. Good stories, bad stories, funny stories, you name it. They spend a great deal of time and energy finding childcare so the kids can stay at home, and then on their date, the kids dominate the conversation! There's nothing inherently wrong with this, of course. Everyone likes telling stories about their children. But if you get to the end of the night and realize you know everything there is to know about the other couple's children but very little about the couple, you've probably spent too much time on the joys and challenges of childrearing.

Activity: The rules for a double date are similar to those for your regular dates: (1) do something *fun*, and (2) if possible, try something none of you have done before. Just as you and your spouse build intimacy through these types of activities, you can also, as a couple, build stronger, deeper friendships by experiencing them with other couples. So go out and try some exotic food. Play laser tag or go swing dancing. Be creative and stretch your boundaries!

Questions: Ask questions and tell stories that will give you greater insights into the lives of your friends. For example, tell them your story, and let them tell you theirs. Even if you've known the other couple for years, you might not know some of the finer details of their dating, their wedding, and so on. Spend time reminiscing and sharing stories.

If you're part of the same babysitting co-op, or even if you and the other couple have made a commitment to regular date nights, compare notes. What are some favorite dates you've been on recently? What are some of your favorite places in town to go on a date?

If you share the same beliefs, don't be afraid to broach spiritual matters. What have you been learning in church lately? What have you been studying in a small group? Individually? As a couple?

Connect

Communication's never been as easy as today, and it
would make me happy when you've gone so far away,
if you'd send me an e-mail that says "I love you."
—Pet Shop Boys, "E-mail"

Earlier in the chapter we talked about the importance of maximizing
everyday moments—of creating opportunities to build intimacy not
only during dates but amid the hustle and bustle of everyday life. We
divided a typical day into three sections (when you're together in the
early morning, when you're apart at midday, and when you're back
together in the evening). This date is designed to help you hone your
communication skills during the middle part of the day—those hours
when you're typically apart because of work, school, and so on.

Technology has made it easier than ever before for husbands and
wives to stay connected throughout the day. Smartphones, iPads, free
wi-fi at restaurants, Skype, texting, email—in most cases you'd have
to work really hard to find yourself in a situation that would prohibit
you from sending a brief "I love you" to your spouse either in real time
or in the form of a message he or she can read later.

Activity: Have a high-tech treasure hunt in which the treasure
you're looking for is . . . each other! Go somewhere you can use your
electronic devices to full advantage, preferably a shopping center with
free wi-fi. Then split up. After twenty minutes or so, contact each
other through texts or phone calls. Leave clues as to your whereabouts
(e.g., "I'm standing in a store with a bright-blue logo," or "I can see the

main entrance from where I'm standing"). Can your partner figure out where you're at? If you're really adventurous and have a capable device, use Skype or FaceTime to communicate visually. Can your partner figure out where you're at by spotting clues that might be visible over your shoulder? Have fun using your electronic devices to track each other down. Once you've found your prize (i.e., each other), celebrate by going somewhere fun for dessert.

Questions: After your activity, discuss some ways you can stay better connected during the hours you're apart throughout the week. If the focus of your date was maximizing everyday moments (see date 26, "Stolen Moments"), recall some of that discussion. Here are some ideas for staying connected:

- Send an occasional email or text to say "I love you and I'm thinking about you."
- Write a nice message on your spouse's Facebook page.
- Call on your way home from work and ask, "Is there anything I can pick up for you at the store?"
- Call your spouse during a time you know he or she won't be able to answer the phone, and leave a romantic voice mail.
- Use Skype or FaceTime to say hi to each other visually.
- Meet for lunch.
- When practical to do so, drop by your spouse's office with a special treat (e.g., a cup of coffee, a snack) and say hi to colleagues and coworkers.
- Email or text a quick snapshot of what you're doing right now . . . even if it's just sitting at your desk at work or cutting vegetables at home.

We're the Best of Friends

This is my lover, this [is] my friend.
—Song of Songs 5:16

Are you and your spouse *friends*? Many couples wouldn't even consider that question, because they see themselves as *more* than friends. They view "friend" and "spouse" as two distinct categories. And in some ways, this is true. Google defines *friend* as "a person whom one knows and with whom one has a bond of mutual affection, typically exclusive of sexual or family relations."[26] Your spouse is both your lover and a member of your family, so that definition couldn't possibly apply. At a stretch, you might be able to consider your mate your "friend with benefits," as tacky as that sounds.

But let's consider some other definitions of friendship. *Merriam-Webster* defines *friend* as "one attached to another by affection or esteem."[27] That sounds a bit more marital, doesn't it? And while not strictly a definition, we like what C. S. Lewis said on the matter: "It is when we are doing things together that friendship springs up—painting, sailing ships, praying, philosophizing, fighting shoulder to shoulder. Friends look in the same direction."[28]

In an article for Focus on the Family, Alyson Weasley suggests that friendship is among the most important components of marriage and summarizes twelve ways that couples can cultivate it:

1. Recognize that friendship building takes a lot of work—and time. Cut the fat out of your day.

2. Establish a time each week to spend quality time together—then guard that time with your lives! [Well said, Alyson. That's what this book is about!]

3. Choose to spend time together rather than apart. This may mean sacrificing good things for a season, such as small groups, ministry, or bonding time with guys or gals.

4. Explore the interests of your spouse, be it baseball, art, musical theater, gardening, or hunting. Find out what they are passionate about and then join them. Often this takes a bit of sacrifice.

5. Take time to find common interests and then engage in them.

6. Use conflict to sharpen and purify friendship.

7. Nourish and care for one another. Be gentle with one another.

8. Accountability and mutual respect, including in the areas of sexuality, finances, and relationships, should be priorities.

9. Establish daily habits, especially praying together.

10. Affirm one another every day. Be intentional in communicating the other's strengths.

11. Be transparent with one another.

12. Communicate. Most experts agree that regular communication builds a friendship that weathers the storms of life.[29]

Did you notice anything about that list? That's right! You've been putting many of those principles into practice already through regular dating. You've committed to regular dates (point 2), you've explored your spouse's interests (point 4), you've cultivated common interests (point 5), you've learned to nourish each other (point 7), you've endeavored to deepen your spiritual bond (point 9), and you've made attempts to maximize everyday moments (points 9 and 10). Perhaps you and your spouse are better friends than you realize!

Activity: Pick an activity that reinforces one of the concepts from Alyson Weasley's list. If you've already taken part in the "Shared Interests" date from earlier in the chapter (date 7), perhaps you could engage in the same shared activity again. Or choose another activity you both enjoy. Have fun!

Questions: After your activity, talk about what friendship means to you in the context of your marriage. Whom did you consider your best friend as a child? In what ways is having a same-sex best friend similar to having me as your best friend? In what ways is it different? What qualities do you see as essential in a friend? How can we work to forge stronger bonds of friendship in our marriage?

Dream Maker

*A dream you dream alone may be a dream, but
a dream two people dream together is a reality.*
—Yoko Ono, *Grapefruit: A Book
of Instructions and Drawings*

Do you still have dreams—goals in life that you'd like to achieve? For many people, dreams are the stuff of youth. By the time they get married and start raising kids, they feel they need to set those dreams aside in the interest of family. If they can successfully navigate their kids through childhood and adolescence without any serious bouts with the law, and if they can weather that same period with their marriage still reasonably intact, they've achieved their "dream." But we all know this wasn't our dream when we got married. These are important and valuable things but definitely not the extent of the marriage we always dreamed of.

Certainly, having a healthy family should be among your top priorities. And there's no denying that some things need to be set aside when one makes the transition from single to married life. If your dream in college was to be the world's greatest Xbox champion or to have the country's largest collection of expensive designer shoes, you probably don't want to carry those youthful pursuits into your marriage. Far too many marriages and families have suffered as the result of someone's dream becoming a self-centered and unhealthy obsession.

At the same time, there's no reason to completely abandon your dreams when you get married, so long as those desires don't interfere with your pursuit of God or harm your relationships with those you love. Neither should having dreams and aspirations be the business only of young people. Consider the following:[30]

- Andrea Bocelli didn't start singing opera until he was thirty-four. Some "experts" told him it was too late to begin an opera career. [By the way, if you're looking to add some romantic music to your repertoire, be sure to download some of this guy's music. There are few things as romantic as love songs performed in Italian!]

- Famous chef Julia Child didn't learn to cook until she was almost forty and didn't launch her popular TV show until she was fifty.

- Laura Ingalls Wilder began writing as a columnist in her forties, and her popular Little House books were written and published when she was in her sixties!

The bottom line is that you're never too old to pursue a dream—and the pursuit of that dream doesn't necessarily have to upset the balance of your precious family. It's something for you and your spouse to think about together.

Activity: One of the basic tenets of this book is that you should try new and exciting things on your dates. But think a little harder about it this time. Is there something that either of you has always wanted to try? If it's doable within the context of a few hours allotted for your date, *go for it*! Or maybe your dream is bigger . . . something that can't be accomplished during a date. That's okay too. Just pick a fun activity and then discuss the logistics of your big dream later.

Questions: After your activity, go someplace quiet and discuss your dreams and aspirations. Explore these questions: Are there things you set aside when we got married that you'd like to consider pursuing? Is it wise to pursue them now? Is it possible? If so, how can I support you in achieving those dreams?

Your dream could be something as simple as learning how to sew or cook or as grandiose as owning property on a lake or going on a trip around the world. Remember, even if some of your dreams aren't attainable in the foreseeable future, sharing them with each other and supporting one another will help build intimacy between you.

Minding Your "Please" and "Thank-Yous"

Manners are a sensitive awareness of the feelings of others. If you have that awareness, you have good manners, no matter what fork you use.

—Emily Post

Let's hearken back once more to the young man and woman at the beginning of this book—the excited young couple who are getting ready for their date. It's safe to say they're putting their best foot forward when it comes to their impending time together. They've spent time making themselves presentable, and they're kind and courteous to each other. Their dating relationship probably wouldn't go very far if she turned up at the front door wearing sweatpants, or if he failed to open doors for her. No matter how laid-back they might be in their personalities, there's something to be said for behaving in a ladylike and gentlemanly manner.

Sadly, in many marriages these basic principles of mannered behavior fly out the window. By the time you've been married to someone for five years, you've pretty much seen it all. You've watched your spouse throw up. You hear him or her snore—loudly—every night. Plus, you might be partners in parenthood now, and everyone knows there isn't time for silly things like holding the door and putting your napkin in your lap when you're busy wrangling children, right?

Wrong! It isn't always easy, but there's no reason why you can't practice reasonably good manners with your spouse even during the sometimes rough childrearing years. If your next-door neighbor comes over to borrow a hammer, you have no problem speaking politely to him. Why can't you do the same with your wife? If you have friends over for dinner, you dab the corners of your mouth and say, "Please pass the salt." Why can't you facilitate the same level of decorum when it's just you and the family around the table?

Emily Post's quote says it all. By practicing good manners, you're sending a message to your spouse (and other loved ones) that says, "I care about your feelings."

Activity: If your budget allows, go somewhere fancy for dinner— a place where good manners are expected. Or try the ballet, opera, or another venue where a certain decorum is expected. Act the way you did when you were first dating. Impress your spouse with your thoughtfulness and consideration!

Questions: Either over dinner or after your activity, discuss the following questions: When a man holds the door for a woman, is that courteous or sexist? Was your family big on manners and decorum? How did that make you feel? How can we encourage good manners in our home without obsessing about it or majoring in the minors? How important are manners amid the craziness of everyday life? What are some other things I can do to show you that I care about your feelings?

Remembering Again . . .

I can see you, your brown skin shining
in the sun. You got your hair combed
back and your sunglasses on, baby.
—Don Henley, "The Boys of Summer"

We've talked at length about the importance of making *reminiscing* a prominent feature of your dates. Remembering special times together can help reawaken feelings of young love and can also help you look forward to future good times as a couple. Opening the floodgates of your shared memories enables you to laugh together, cry together, and feel more intimate.

A music group that was popular during the eighties, when Erin and I (Greg) were in high school, came to Colorado Springs. I thought this would make a great date-night surprise, so I bought tickets. We had a wonderful dinner at a restaurant we'd never been to before. Later we found ourselves in the concert hall, snuggling and reminiscing about our high school days. Suddenly the group played a familiar song.

"I love this song," I said to Erin.

"Me, too," she enthusiastically replied.

Then she moved even closer to me. I was loving this!

I instantly had this moment of clarity, and my mind was flooded with nostalgic memories. But there was one memory, in particular, that I wanted to share with my wife. I turned and whispered in her ear, "Remember that time we were first dating, and this song came on the car radio?" Erin looked into my eyes and nodded. This was perfect. "And then we pulled off into a parking lot and started to smooch," I said. I was rolling now. "Do you remember that?"

"What a great memory," Erin lovingly responded, "but that wasn't me."

Ouch! I think the moral of the story is that if you're going to reminisce about making out, just make sure your wife was there!

For this date, you're going to spend more time reminiscing, but with a more specific focus. You're going to *re-create* a favorite date from before your marriage!

Activity: You may need to discuss a few possibilities before actually embarking on your date. Talk about some of your favorite dates from your courtship period, and then pick one to re-create together. It won't be possible to re-create every last detail, but be as creative as you can to evoke memories of your chosen date. Do you still have any of the clothes you wore on your date (assuming you can still fit in them)? Even if you can't remember the exact clothes, perhaps you could get a little crazy by taking a trip to Goodwill in advance of your date and finding some now-out-of-style clothes from the eighties, nineties, or beyond, or whenever your dating glory days occurred. Are any nearby restaurants similar to the one you visited on your favorite date?

Questions: After your activity, go someplace quiet to debrief and discuss the following questions: Do you think we were successful in re-creating our chosen date? How did it make you feel? Do we have differing recollections about the details of our original date? In addition to the date we just re-created, what are some of your other favorite dating memories from before we married?

Accentuating the Positive

I could list a million things
I love to like about you.

—"I Love the Way You Love Me,"
performed by John Michael Montgomery

Although this book is about the benefits of marital dating, we've repeatedly stressed that *every day* presents you with the opportunity to connect with your spouse and pursue intimacy. Having couple time alone is important, but it's equally critical to maximize those everyday moments to bless your spouse and invest in your relationship.

Hopefully there are little things, simple things, you do for each other on a regular basis that communicate your love. We're not talking about bringing home a surprise bouquet or cooking an elaborate, favorite meal. It might be simply taking a few minutes away from the iPad and the TV to just sit and talk with your spouse about the day's events. Or perhaps you help with getting the kids bathed and in bed so your spouse can have a little downtime. Maybe you put the occasional "I love you" note in your spouse's lunch box. Or you offer a massage at the end of the day, even though you're bone tired too.

The purpose of this date is simple. Think about the little things your spouse does every day that communicate love to you. Make a list of those things and then share it with your spouse.

Activity: Prior to the date, compile your list. It doesn't have to be extensive. List just two or three things your spouse does that you appreciate and that make you feel loved. Then engage in a fun date-night activity. Go out for a nice dinner. Spend some time perusing the racks at your favorite bookshop. Take a relaxing walk around the park.

Questions: After your activity, go someplace quiet and exchange the lists you made. Discuss the following questions: Were you surprised by any of the things on my list? Why or why not? What are some other little things I can do to bless you and make you feel loved?

The Learning Curve

*It's what you learn after you
know it all that counts.*
—John Wooden, *Wooden on Leadership*

If you think back to your school days (whether elementary, high school, or college), you know the benefits of learning in a group setting. Perhaps you had a favorite study group or study partner to help you grasp certain concepts and ideas. When it came time for that algebra test, you were on your own. But you didn't get to that point on your own. The preparation involved intense study with your friends or classmates, maybe even your parents. Learning is often a very communal process.

After graduation, many people assume that the time of learning—at least in a formal setting—has ended. They achieve their degree and see no reason to continue exploring the world around them or expanding their knowledge. But that need not be the case. Just as there is always something more to learn about your spouse, there's always something more to learn about the world outside your door. If God has gifted you with a natural affinity for science, mathematics, or the arts, it would be a shame for you to put those gifts on the shelf simply because you're no longer a full-time student.

Because learning is a communal process, is there a specific subject you and your spouse are both interested in that you could study together? Learning a new skill or expanding your knowledge of a specific subject is another great way for you to build intimacy!

Activity: Take a class, attend a seminar, read an educational book, or visit a museum together. Find a subject that interests you both and expand your knowledge as a couple. Here are some possibilities:

- Take a pottery or woodworking class together.
- Attend a community lecture series.
- In the days leading up to your date, read a book on a subject that interests you and then discuss it on your date night.
- Visit a museum and explore an area of science or history that interests you.
- Watch a documentary and then discuss it afterward.
- Go stargazing together. Download an astronomy app for your phone that will help you identify constellations and other celestial bodies.

Questions: After your activity, discuss your experience together, asking the following questions: What did you learn during the course of our date? How can we continue to work together to expand our knowledge of our chosen subject? Are there other subjects we can explore together as a couple? How can we make learning fun?

Something New

*A mind that is stretched by a new experience
can never go back to its old dimensions.*
—Oliver Wendell Holmes

One of the basic tenets of marital dating is to find new and exciting experiences for you to enjoy together as a couple. Trying new activities, rather than simply repeating the same old things date after date, is a great way to re-create those feelings of excitement and discovery you experienced when you were first dating and getting to know each other.

While we've encouraged you to try new things throughout this book, make that your top priority for this date. Earlier in the chapter we suggested doing something together that you've always wanted to do. This time, try something that you may not have even considered before. Get creative. Stretch your boundaries. Step outside your comfort zone. Don't be afraid to embrace something that lies far outside the realm of what you'd normally consider a dating activity. Enjoy the thrill of making a new discovery together!

Activity: Try something truly new to both of you. Go back through some of the suggested dates earlier in this chapter (see the lists in dates 7, 21, or 25, for example) and pick a new activity or consider some of these suggestions:

- Go on a hot-air balloon ride.
- Go on a scavenger hunt. Pick a location and take your smartphones. Create a list of items and start taking pictures. The

first person to capture a photo of every item on the list wins! (For example, go to a mall or superstore and take pics of a desk lamp, a bag of dog food, and a roll of paper towels. Or go to the park and shoot photos of park benches, a squirrel, people taking walks, etc.)

- Try indoor rock climbing.
- Rent Segways (you know, those sci-fi looking, two-wheeled cycles—*segway.com*) and tour the neighborhood, a park, and other locations.
- Drive to a neighboring town or city and eat at the most obscure, unconventional-looking restaurant you can find.

Questions: After your activity, discuss the following questions: As a child, were you afraid to try new things? Why or why not? How did it feel for you to step out of your comfort zone for our date? Was our chosen activity something we'd like to repeat in the future? What are some ways we can keep a spirit of discovery and adventure in our marriage? How can we avoid getting stuck in a rut?

Grace Given, Grace Received

What once was hurt, what once was friction;
what left a mark no longer stings, because
Grace makes beauty out of ugly things.
—U2, "Grace"

Grace is one of the most commonly used words in the Christian vernacular. The "Sunday school" definition of the word is usually something along the lines of "God's unmerited favor." *Merriam-Webster* defines it as "unmerited divine assistance given humans for their regeneration or sanctification," with the secondary definition "disposition to or an act or instance of kindness, courtesy or clemency."[31]

Both of those definitions have profound implications for Christian marriage. Essentially, as those who have received God's unmerited favor, we are to emulate Christ by extending kindness and clemency to all we encounter, whether our spouse, our kids, our coworkers, or strangers.

Often it seems hardest to give and receive grace within our own families. It's easier to be forbearing and forgiving toward strangers and acquaintances—people we don't see on a consistent basis—than it is to demonstrate grace toward those who live under the same roof with us. In many ways, familiarity really does breed contempt!

Dr. Harold L. Arnold Jr., the founder of Discovering Family International, has developed a unique acrostic that helps married couples extend grace to each other. Here's how it breaks down:

Give your spouse the benefit of the doubt.

Risk being honest [with yourself and with your spouse].

Accept your spouse's feelings at face value.

Complain without criticizing [don't belittle your spouse].

Embrace your differences.[32]

That's a great picture of G-R-A-C-E in marriage! But since we've already established that your date nights aren't for administrating your relationship or for hashing out controversial or contentious issues, how might you incorporate G-R-A-C-E into your precious few hours of couple time? The answer is that you can accentuate the positive— talk about the ways your spouse is already excelling in extending grace in your relationship. This doesn't mean that your spouse is perfect or that there aren't areas you both need to work on. Extending grace simply means encouraging each other, lifting one another up, and agreeing to talk about the areas that need work at a later time.

Activity: Feel free to engage in a typical date-night activity, so long as it's fun and exciting. If you want to do something more in line with the grace theme, consider finding a book on the Christian concept of grace and reading it in the days leading up to your date. Then discuss it during your time together. We'd recommend Philip Yancey's *What's So Amazing about Grace?* as a good resource.[33]

Questions: After your activity, find a quiet coffee shop or another relaxing venue to discuss the following questions: How would you define *grace*? Why is it so important? How can we extend grace to each other? To our children? To our extended family? In other relationships? Remember to keep your responses uplifting, positive, and encouraging. If you feel that your spouse is falling short in certain areas, save that discussion for another time.

Cooking Up Something Fun

*Some people like to paint pictures, or do gardening,
or build a boat in the basement. Other people get
a tremendous pleasure out of the kitchen, because
cooking is just as creative and imaginative an
activity as drawing, or wood carving, or music.*

—Julia Child, in Lynn Gilbert's
Particular Passions

Here's another chance for a stay-at-home date. Earlier in the chapter we outlined a home date that involved ordering a take-out meal. This time you're going to work together to make the meal.

Now, don't worry. We realize that in most homes, one person is usually in charge of the lion's share of the cooking. And in homes in which cooking is a shared responsibility between husband and wife, it's rare that both spouses will work extensively on the same meal *together*. But that's what you're going to do for this date. You're going to find a new dish that neither of you has cooked before. Then you're going to work together to create that dish! To be honest, it's okay if the dish you select looks a little bit intimidating on paper. The more complex the better! Why? Because cooking an exotic meal together reinforces several of the important components of marital dating, in-cluding (1) working together as a team; (2) stepping outside of your comfort zone and the routine, mundane activities you're accustomed to; and (3) doing something new and exciting.

As you work on your meal together, don't feel pressure to create something worthy of *MasterChef* or a show on the Food Network. It's okay if the risotto is a tad squishy or the salad dressing isn't quite tangy enough. The goal is to have *fun* working together and creating something beautiful.

Activity: Pick your new recipe—maybe something exotic or ethnic. If time allows, go to the store together and pick out the freshest ingredients beforehand. And remember that there are plenty of unique recipes built upon basic ingredients, too. There's no need to buy rare and exotic (i.e., *expensive*) ingredients to create a new recipe. Go online to find recipe ideas. If you're feeling especially insecure about creating a new dish together, YouTube contains hundreds of step-by-step cooking videos from both professional and amateur chefs. Watching some of these user-friendly clips can help give you the boost of confidence you need to create your own masterpiece!

Questions: While enjoying your meal together, discuss the following questions: Do you like this recipe? Are there some other recipes we could try together? How do you feel we performed as a team on this project? Would this experience have been different if one person cooked the meal alone, as opposed to us working on it together? Did our differing personalities help or hinder the end result (i.e., one person being a stickler for detailed measurements and strict adherence to the recipe versus the other's willingness to just add a "pinch" of salt and venture outside the parameters of the recipe)? Did you learn anything about me during this process of making a meal together?

date **40**

Tenderness

*She has her griefs and care, but the soft words, they
are spoke so gentle, it makes it easier, easier to bear.*

—"Try a Little Tenderness,"
performed by Otis Redding

Think about your typical weekday. It's likely full of challenges and
frustrations, from rush-hour traffic to obnoxious coworkers to meet-
ings with the school principal for an unruly child to car trouble, and
on and on. The hours during the day when you're apart can be devas-
tating to your self-esteem, your attitude, and your faith in humanity.
It's a tough world out there.

On those especially trying days, how do you treat your spouse
when the family finally arrives back together under the same roof? Are
you snarky? Do you take the cares and frustrations of the day out on
your spouse and kids? Is venting about your own day more important
to you than empathizing with your spouse about his or her day?

I (Greg) remember one time when Erin was out with a friend.
Like typical women, they had returned from their girls' night out and
were now sitting in the driveway talking. As if they hadn't just spent
the entire evening doing that!

I had eaten something for dinner that didn't agree with me. As a
matter of fact, I have a particular food allergy, to some type of preser-
vative, and when I eat it, I go into anaphylactic shock. This is when
you experience diarrhea, vomiting, bronchospasm, and breathing
problems. Very fun!

All of a sudden, my lips and tongue started to swell, and I was having a hard time breathing. I really thought I was in trouble. So I quickly found an old EpiPen and went in search of Erin. Since she's a nurse, she's usually the one who handles the family medical emergencies. She was still sitting with her friend in the car when I walked up holding the EpiPen. I'm not sure what tipped Erin off that I was in trouble, but it could have been my swollen tongue or the large needle I was holding in my hand.

Erin rushed to me and grabbed the EpiPen. She sat me down on a chair, and with both hands gripping the large needle, she raised it above her head. Then, with the strength of Atlas himself, she started stabbing me in the leg. Unfortunately for me, the ancient EpiPen took awhile to discharge the life-giving epinephrine. But I was saved!

What does this have to do with tenderness? Like that EpiPen, some days after work, it feels as if my words stab at my family. When I'm worn-out and exhausted, I'm short with my words, and I want to just hole up in my man cave alone. Of course, that's no way to maintain healthy relationships with those who are closest to me.

The book of Proverbs reminds us that "a gentle answer turns away wrath, but a harsh word stirs up anger" (15:1). This is a crucial principle for husbands and wives who have hurried, harried lives (in other words, *every* husband and wife). After a stress-filled day, your time together should be filled with tenderness. Your home should be a place of *refuge* from the trials and challenges of life—not a place to magnify and amplify them. This doesn't mean you should bury your own frustrations and cares down deep. But it does mean that you and your spouse should endeavor to empathize with one another, to hear each other out before launching into your own diatribe about the day's frustrations. Adopting this approach will help you share each other's burdens. This is one of the reasons why Scripture encourages us to "carry each other's burdens, and in this way you will fulfill the law of Christ" (Galatians 6:2) and admonishes us to "be quick to listen, slow to speak and slow to become angry" (James 1:19).

Activity: As usual, try something new and exciting. Whatever your activity, make sure to *listen* to your spouse and *empathize* with him or her. You might want to consider a quieter activity, without a lot of distractions and stimulation, that affords you the opportunity to zero in and focus on one another. Convey tenderness toward your mate throughout the evening. We often think of tenderness as something a man demonstrates toward a woman. But it's important to remember that wives can and should demonstrate tenderness toward their husbands, too.

Questions: Either during your activity or in a quiet location afterward, discuss the following questions: What things do I do that communicate *tenderness* toward you? Are there other ways I can communicate tenderness on a regular basis? Were your parents tender toward each other? How? Especially after long, tough days, how can we make a concerted effort to reconnect and show tenderness and empathy?

Community-Minded

How far that little candle throws his beams!
So shines a good deed in a naughty world.
—Portia, in William Shakespeare's
The Merchant of Venice

Up to this point, the majority of dates outlined in this book have been introspective, focused on fostering intimacy between you and your spouse, to help you "turn toward" each other (see chapter 2). That will always be an important part of your marriage. However, all of us, whether married or single, can sometimes carry this concept too far. We can become so focused on bettering ourselves, our marriages, and our children that we become self-absorbed. We get so busy navel-gazing that we fail to see the world around us.

That's why it's important for couples—especially Christian couples—to look for opportunities to serve others together. There's something beautiful about husbands and wives working together to invest time and energy in loving and serving others. Some have described this as a "missional marriage."

But remember, without proper barriers and safeguards in place, reaching out to others can cause your own relationship to suffer. Too many men and women in professional ministry have seen their own marriages and families crumble as a result of being too focused on others. The key is finding the proper balance between nurturing your own relationship and investing in the lives of others.

Once that balance has been found, the blessings of reaching out to others as a husband-wife team are numerous. Susan Mathis writes,

> Serving as a couple has benefits that go beyond bonding, contentment and peace. There's a sweet intimacy that comes with working together on a service project or giving together to those in need. . . . Participating together in ministry opportunities—whether in your church, neighborhood, community or the world—can also help you to grow in your faith as a couple. Working side-by-side to fulfill the Great Commission—in whatever capacity—deepens your spiritual intimacy like little else can. . . . But in the end, it's not really about you, is it? It's about them—the poor, the needy, those who need a touch from God. Serving others strengthens the infrastructure of your church, your neighborhood, your community and the world. It transforms lives—theirs and yours—and brings people together. Whenever you serve others, you become the hands and feet of your Savior. You change lives.[34]

We couldn't have said it better ourselves! For this date, you're going to experience the joy and satisfaction of reaching out to someone in your neighborhood, church, or community.

Activity: Do a good deed for someone else! Look for opportunities to serve in your community. Here are a few ideas:

- Volunteer at a local soup kitchen or homeless shelter.
- Host a coat drive or clothing drive at your church.

- Help rake leaves, shovel snow, or otherwise beautify a neighbor's yard.
- Volunteer at your local library to help underprivileged kids learn to read or to help non-English speakers learn English.

Need more ideas? Here are some additional activities—some of which can be incorporated into a date night, and some of which involve a longer-term commitment—courtesy of Samantha Krieger and StartMarriageRight.com:

1. *Open up your home.* Invite non-Christians in your workplace, neighborhood, or kids' school over for dinner. Feed them well and get to know them on a deeper level. Talk about your marriage and what God is doing in your life. Your kindness and hospitality will speak volumes.

2. *Put down the phone and pull out the earplugs.* We're a "plugged in" generation, and we're all guilty of tuning out. But in order to know what the needs are around us, we can't be distracted by technology. Be fully present with the people around you (including your spouse!).

3. *Engage your server.* When you're out on a dinner date, let your server be a part of your relationship. Get to know him or her by asking questions. Find out if your server has any needs, and if you feel led, pray for him or her and share the gospel. Don't forget to leave a good tip!

4. *Volunteer at local organizations and nonprofits.* These organizations exist all around your town/city and are usually in need of solid volunteers. And better yet—married couples. Seek out an organization that you and your spouse are both passionate about.

5. *Prepare and deliver a meal.* Be watchful of who might be going through a crisis or simply struggling. Double up on a recipe one evening and give the other half away. Rally your friends to contribute by creating a Care Calendar for the person/family in need.

6. *Consider becoming a foster couple or adopting.* Invest in the life of a child who desperately needs a loving home.

7. *Plan to attend local events.* Especially during the holidays, there are tons of festivals and celebrations going on. Check out your city's website to see what's going on, and mark your calendar to attend something fun. Go with the purpose of reaching out to someone.

8. *Carry extra change.* When you're going shopping, keep extra change in your pockets with the intention of giving it away. Chances are you will run into a homeless person who can use it more than you.

9. *Start a playgroup.* Our community group started a playgroup that consisted of all the moms. We would meet randomly at local places like Chick-fil-A, the park, or the mall. We would get together and meet every other week at a different house. It was a great way to reach out and encourage fellow moms.

10. *Create an interest group or club.* What are you passionate about? Photography, running, football, quilting, going green? Invite a few people who love what you do, and do that thing together! You'll have a blast doing what you love and reaching out.[35]

Questions: After your service activity, go someplace quiet to unwind and discuss the following questions: How do you feel about the service project we just completed together? Was your own family involved in community service? If so, was it considered an obligation or a privilege? How critical is it for Christians to be involved in acts of service? How can we make acts of love and service a regular part of our marriage and family life rather than just isolated, one-time events?

Trust

*You can trust us to stick with you through
thick and thin—to the bitter end. And you
can trust us to keep any secret of yours—closer
than you keep it yourself. But you cannot trust
us to let you face trouble alone, and go off
without a word. We are your friends, Frodo.*

—Merry to Frodo in J. R. R. Tolkien's
The Fellowship of the Ring

A few years ago, during a date at our favorite restaurant, Erin began sharing about how exhausted she gets while dealing with our children all day (our oldest is now in college). "Sometimes during the day, I feel like I'm losing my mind!" she said at one point. We ended up laughing about how chaotic parenting can be at times, and we even referred to her as "Crazy Mama."

However, on the way home, we ended up having an argument about a sensitive topic. (Yeah, we obviously didn't follow our own advice about not allowing contentious issues to intrude on our dates!) During the argument, I (Greg) made a rather ill-advised comment, suggesting that the argument was Erin's fault because she wasn't thinking clearly. "Remember dinner?" I said. "You've already admitted that you're losing your mind!"

Ouch! That statement caused Erin to lose a bit of trust in me as a friend. Not only was the comment not funny, but it also actually weakened our relationship. Why? Because in the middle of an argument, I used something against Erin that she'd shared during an intimate conversation. Nobody wants to reveal private and sacred information when it might later be used against them during a time of conflict! When we resort to such thoughtless sarcasm, it undermines trust and hinders open communication. When couples feel unsafe sharing their emotions, their hearts tend to close, and they disconnect emotionally from each other. On the other hand, when people feel safe, they are naturally inclined to open their hearts and spirits, and intimacy occurs effortlessly and naturally.

Activity: There are many levels of trust within marriage—emotional, relational, spiritual, physical, and so on. Consider a fun activity that reinforces the concept of trust between you and your spouse. It could be anything from a ropes course to skydiving to singing karaoke or scaling a climbing wall. Like the teamwork date earlier in the chapter (date 2), it should be an activity that requires you to rely on each other in order to complete—something that requires you to say to one another, "I've got your back."

Questions: After your activity, explore the following questions: Did you trust me during our chosen activity? Would you have done the same thing with someone else? With a stranger? How can we ensure that our marriage is always a safe environment to share private and sensitive information?

Home Date!

Home, where my thought's escaping,
home, where my music's playing, home,
where my love lies waiting . . .
—Simon and Garfunkel, "Homeward Bound"

We've already highlighted some dates in this chapter that lend them-selves to staying at home (the "Passion" and "Cooking Up Something Fun" dates, for example). However, this is a concept that warrants revisiting. For one thing, we know that even in the best of economic times, going out on a regular basis can become an expensive proposi-tion for many couples. Staying at home and spending quality time together after the kids are in bed can be a cost-effective way for couples to build intimacy and "turn toward" each other. For another thing, your home is also, in many ways, the centerpiece of your married and family life. Just as it's sometimes good to get away from a domestic setting to have new and exciting experiences, it's also beneficial to em-brace the comfortable environs of hearth and home as a couple. Such a setting lends itself to fostering connection and intimacy.

Oh, and one more thing. A home date can also serve as a great plan B when your childcare falls through, which will inevitably hap-pen more often than you'd like. Maybe your own kids are sick and unable to be entrusted to the care of a babysitter. Or perhaps the baby-sitter you have lined up realizes she's double-booked and can't keep her commitment. Whatever the case, a last-minute change of plans doesn't automatically mean that your date night has to be canceled.

Sometimes, even when it comes to an unexpected change to your date-night plans, "there's no place like home."

Activity: Just because you're staying home doesn't mean you have to dress like a slob. Get out of those sweatpants and put a little effort into looking nice for your spouse. As for actual activities, use your imagination. For example, once the kids are asleep, go out on your back porch, grill some steaks, and enjoy a gourmet meal under the stars. If it's cold outside, put a tablecloth down in front of the fireplace and enjoy your meal there. If you need help coming up with ideas, just google "home date nights" or something similar, and you'll likely find more ideas than you could possibly use in a lifetime. Here's one interesting set of ideas that we found at, of all places, *huggies.com* (yes, the diaper company!):

> Who says you actually have to go out? Some of the best times can happen in your home sweet home after the kids are asleep.
>
> "My husband and I start planning our night out at the beginning of the week. On the day of our date, I let my daughter skip her nap so she'll go to sleep early. Then [my husband and I] cook together in the kitchen and dine with soft music in the background. We may not be going anywhere fancy, but it's enough for us to enjoy a couple of quiet hours together." (Maureen Smithe, mom of two, Chicago, Illinois)
>
> "I've started making themed 'date boxes.' I'll take a shoebox and fill it with, say, cupcake mix, temporary tattoos, and Pop Rocks for a night of goofing around like kids. We've had such a good time opening the boxes on date night and using what's

in them, I've turned my idea into a business." (Lindsay Christianson, mom of one, Minneapolis, Minnesota)

"Here's the next best thing to a date night: After our kids are in bed on weekdays, my husband and I both sometimes end up in front of our computers with work to do, him upstairs in the TV room and me downstairs in the office. We each turn on iChat and some music, then talk and make each other laugh as we work. It gets us 'face time' until we get the chance to go on a real date." (Juliette Wilson, mom of three, Modesto, California)

"When it's a warm evening out, my husband and I like to take that day's newspaper, a magazine or two, and whatever books we're reading out to our porch. We read and catch up, usually with my feet propped up on his lap. It's pretty much the opposite of a hot date, but we love it." (Barbara Turnmire, mom of two, Provo, Utah)[36]

Questions: If your chosen activity doesn't allow it, make sure you reserve some time afterward to connect through good conversation. Catch up on the events of the day and the week. Ask yourselves, "Are there other ways we can foster intimacy in our relationship on a regular basis when we're at home?

Family Date

Rejoice with your family in the
beautiful land of life!
—Albert Einstein, letter to
Paul Ehrenfest, June 1918

Once again, it's time to break from the traditional marital-dating template. Instead of enjoying quiet, uninterrupted couple time, you're going to involve the entire family in your date! This isn't something you should do frequently (couple time should remain a priority), but there are certainly benefits to the occasional family outing of this nature.

For one thing, a family date eliminates the need to procure childcare. For once you won't have to worry about paying a babysitter or finding free childcare or worrying about changing your plans at the last minute if your scheduled babysitter falls through.

More important, a family date sets a great example for your kids. It allows you to be affectionate and romantic with each other in their presence. We're not talking about "making out" in front of them—gross! However, it's entirely appropriate for husbands and wives to show affection for each other in front of their kids, and it's actually a very good thing for kids to see. It demonstrates a healthy male-female dynamic and sends the message that married life can be *fun*—it's not just drudgery and arguing over bills.

Dr. Ken R. Canfield, founder of the National Center for Fathering, explains how marital dating can make a dramatic impact on your children:

Your son is taking subconscious notes. He's asking, "How should I treat women?" "What does it mean to be a husband?" Your daughter also has her eye on you. The thought of giving herself to a man in marriage can be frightening. She's asking herself how well her mother fared in the deal. Your children watch when you open car doors for your wife. They listen closely when you compliment her on how radiant she looks in that new dress, or express your appreciation for all she does for you.[37]

Activity: Choose a Saturday or another time when both you and the kids are free and engage in something fun. Don't be afraid to call it a "family date." Many of the same principles apply. It's a chance to get away, invest in one another, and form deeper bonds. Go to a new restaurant, drive to a neighboring town to see the sights, play miniature golf or Frisbee golf, take a picnic to the park, go sightseeing at some local landmarks, and so on.

Questions: After the date is over and it's just the two of you again—perhaps at night in bed—discuss the day's family date. Consider the following questions: Did your parents go on dates when you were young? Did they model a healthy marriage for you? Can our own commitment to marital dating model healthy marriage concepts for our kids? What are some ways we can maximize everyday moments with our children in the same way we've endeavored to do in our marriage?

With Thanksgiving

In everyone's life, at some time, our inner fire
goes out. It is then burst into flame by an
encounter with another human being. We
should all be thankful for those people who
rekindle the inner spirit.
—Albert Schweitzer

At Thanksgiving we set aside time to reflect on the blessings God has given us—our families, our friends, our health, our jobs, our freedom. These are all tremendous gifts. But during significant events like the Thanksgiving holiday, we tend to look at the big picture—attempting to acknowledge *all* of the many blessings God has given us rather than narrowing in on specifics.

This is especially true when it comes to our spouses. It's one thing to say, "Thank You, God, for my wonderful wife," while everyone is sitting around the dinner table. That's a nice gesture, but let's be honest; it's not very specific, and besides, it's what everyone expects you to say. So it's important that you also take time alone with your spouse to tell him or her directly *why* you're thankful. This should involve not only thanking God but also thanking your partner—*directly* and *specifically*—for the things he or she does that bless and enrich your life. Throughout the year, we should make a concerted effort to express gratitude *for* our spouses and *to* our spouses!

There's one caveat, however. We must be careful to avoid what pastor John Piper calls "the debtor's ethic." Being thankful for your husband or wife shouldn't involve attempts to pay him or her back for the wonderful things they've done for you. That's not gratitude. Piper explains:

> There is an impulse in the fallen human heart—all our hearts—to forget that gratitude is a spontaneous response of joy to receiving something over and above what we paid for. When we forget this, what happens is that gratitude starts to be misused and distorted as an impulse to pay for the very thing that came to us "gratis." This terrible moment is the birthplace of the "debtor's ethic."
>
> The debtor's ethic says, "Because you have done something good for me, I feel indebted to do something good for you." This impulse is not what gratitude was designed to produce. God meant gratitude to be a spontaneous expression of pleasure in the gift and the good will of another. He did not mean it to be an impulse to return favors. If gratitude is twisted into a sense of debt, it gives birth to the debtor's ethic—and the effect is to nullify grace.[38]

Piper is talking here primarily about our tendency as believers to try to pay God back for His grace to us (as if that were possible!). But the same principle applies to marriage. True gratitude toward your spouse won't take the form of paying him or her back or returning the favor. Instead, it will be an honest, joyous expression of love and thankfulness for what you could never repay.

Activity: With Thanksgiving drawing near—and the frantic preparations it likely entails for you—use this opportunity to go someplace quiet and relaxing for dinner. Find a restaurant that doesn't have *anything* on the menu resembling turkey and dressing!

Questions: Either over dinner or in a quiet location afterward, take turns sharing *specific* reasons why you're thankful for your mate. Make a list if you feel it would be helpful. Here are some ways you might complete the sentence "I'm thankful for you because . . ."

I have someone to share my life with.

I have someone to help balance me out.

two are better than one; together we're stronger than we are apart.

the ways in which we differ make me a better person by stretching me.

I have someone to laugh with.

I have someone to hold me when life gets hard.

I have someone to come home to.

I have someone to challenge me.

I have someone to hold me accountable.

I have someone to cuddle with!

Once you've made a list of general qualities, dig deeper. Talk about a specific time recently when your spouse made you laugh or otherwise cheered you up. If you're thankful for your spouse's parenting skills, cite a *specific* example of those skills in action. This process has the potential to be a time of great connection, reminiscing, and intimacy.

A Christmas Date

Christmas gift suggestions: To your enemy,
forgiveness. To an opponent, tolerance.
To a friend, your heart. To a customer,
service. To all, charity. To every child,
a good example. To yourself, respect.
—Author unknown

There's no getting around it: Christmas in the twenty-first century is a big business. We'd suggest that the perfect antidote to the crass commercialism and consumerism of Christmas is an attitude of *service*. What better way to take the focus off ourselves and the "stuff" that somehow seems so important at Christmas? The Bible reminds us that "the Son of Man did not come to be served, *but to serve*, and to give his life as a ransom for many" (Matthew 20:28). The Child in the manger is a portrait not of kingly elegance and excess but of humility and service.

This date will give you the opportunity to take a break from the holiday grind and invest *as a couple* in the well-being of someone else. Through volunteering your time and talent in service to others, you'll experience the satisfaction of making a positive impact on an individual, a group, or even your entire community. What's more, you'll likely experience a deeper marital bond and sense of intimacy through serving together.

Your Christmas date can go one of two ways. You might want to simply combine your date and your service project into one event. Or if your crowded holiday calendar allows, you can go on a regular date to plan and talk about your volunteer ideas and then actually perform your act of service at a later time—perhaps on a Saturday. This second approach would allow you to enjoy some quality couple time on your date and then involve your kids in the actual service project later.

Activity: Pick an activity that appeals to both of you (as well as your children, if you choose to involve them). Then *put it on the calendar*! Pick a definite date and time to make your act of service happen so that it won't get lost or overlooked amid the general hustle and bustle of the season. Here are just a few possibilities:

- Volunteer to help with a local toy drive or, if you're really ambitious, initiate a toy drive of your own!
- Volunteer at a soup kitchen or with an organization that collects and distributes coats, hats, and gloves to the homeless.
- Go to a local store and inquire about the possibility of gift-wrapping shoppers' presents for a small donation. Then give the money to a local charity or an organization such as Compassion International or World Vision.
- Do you know someone who will be alone at Christmas? Perhaps there's a widower living nearby or a college student who can't afford to travel home for the holidays. Consider buying a present, baking Christmas cookies, or doing something else to let this person know that he or she is loved. You might even invite this person to take part in your family's own Christmas festivities.
- Gather some friends and family members and go Christmas caroling. Ask local nursing homes and care facilities about the possibility of spending an evening singing Christmas carols for the residents.

- Offer to help neighbors get their home ready for Christmas. Perhaps an older couple or a single-parent family near you could use assistance with shoveling snow, hanging Christmas lights, putting up decorations, or other tasks.

Questions: After your activity, go somewhere quiet for some coffee, hot chocolate, or an eggnog latte and discuss the following questions: What was your all-time favorite Christmas gift? What's the worst Christmas gift you've ever received? What is one of your favorite Christmas memories? What is one gift I can give you this year that doesn't cost money? What Christmas activity do you enjoy most (e.g., looking at Christmas lights, seeing *The Nutcracker*, Christmas shopping)? Growing up, did your family ever engage in an act of service to others around the holidays?

What Are You Doing New Year's Eve?

We were strangers starting out on a journey,
never dreaming what we'd have to go through.
Now here we are, and I'm suddenly
standing at the beginning with you.

—"At the Beginning," performed by
Richard Marx and Donna Lewis in *Anastasia*

Your dating journey has come full circle! If you started with the "New Year's Date" at the beginning of this chapter, you've enjoyed a full year of marital-dating bliss. At least we hope so! Whether you committed to dating once a week, once a month, or some other frequency, the date-night ideas outlined in this chapter (as well as a few special-event dates in the next) have taken you on a journey designed to foster intimacy, connection, excitement, and yes, that word we keep repeating: *fun.*

As the year draws to a close, it's a great time to take stock of what you've learned over the preceding months. Did you set goals for your relationship at the beginning of the year? Did making regular date nights a priority help you achieve those goals? Make this New Year's Eve an opportunity to celebrate where you've been, what you've accomplished, and how you'd like to continue nurturing your relationship in the coming year.

Remember, dating your spouse should remain a regular feature of your marriage for as long as you both shall live. Even if you managed to complete *every* date described in this book over the past year (which is highly unlikely, unless you averaged one date per week all year without fail), there are plenty of dates that are worth repeating two, three, or four times. As we've been saying, there's always something new to learn about your spouse, and engaging in fun date-night activities is a great way to discover those things!

Activity: Go somewhere romantic for New Year's Eve. Have a candlelight dinner. Go dancing. Or if that seems too conventional for you, try something unexpected and different. Grab some fast food and drive up to your favorite romantic overlook. Even if the temperatures outside are frigid, we're sure you can figure out a way to stay warm!

Questions: If you've had quite a few date nights already, take some time to reflect on them and discuss the following questions: Which dates were your favorites? Which ones didn't turn out the way you expected? Which ones would you not care to repeat? How can we continue to make dating a priority in our marriage over the months and years ahead? Finish your date night with prayer, committing your marriage to the Lord for the coming year.

Special Dates for Special Occasions

Whew! That last chapter was l-o-n-g, was it not? Congratulations on navigating successfully through *almost* a year's worth of dates, assuming those dates occurred on a weekly basis. Honestly, most couples would have difficulty keeping up that kind of a pace consistently. So don't feel bad if your schedules and your budget prohibit a once-a-week commitment. So long as you're dating *regularly*, even if it's bimonthly or monthly, you're on the right track.

We know personally how difficult it is to make date nights a regular part of marriage. One time, I (Greg) was trying to get Erin out of the house for our date night. Our four-year-old daughter, Annie, didn't want Mommy to leave. She was crying and had literally wrapped her arms and legs around Erin's leg. I knew that I needed to quickly intervene, or we wouldn't be going out. But before I could say anything to Annie, our ten-year-old son, Garrison, jumped in.

"It's okay," Garrison gently spoke to Annie. "We need to let Mom and Dad go out. This is how they keep their marriage strong." Erin and I were flabbergasted.

Annie released Erin and then asked Garrison, "But what do they do on their date?"

You could instantly tell that Annie had stumped him. He thought about it for a few seconds and then responded, "I'm really not sure. But I think that it ends in kissing." That's my boy!

The point is that we've worked hard to teach our kids that Mom and Dad "must" spend time together without them to keep our marriage strong. When our kids were younger, we would tell them that once we put them down to bed (let's say 7:00 p.m.), that time was now for Mom and Dad to work on our marriage. If they cut into our couple time after seven o'clock (e.g., asking for another drink of water, wanting to say good night for the umpteenth time), we'd make them do chores the next day to make up for the total number of minutes they took from our couple time the previous night.

But back to the subject of a year's worth of dates. In the interest of keeping with that theme, we're going to add a few more date-night ideas to bring us to the magic number of fifty-two dates. Chapter 3, that big, honkin' chapter you just completed, contained forty-seven dates. They included some generic, anytime dates, as well as dates related to specific events common to everyone's calendar: Valentine's Day, Christmas, New Year's, and so on. This chapter contains five additional date ideas.

The dates outlined on the following pages won't differ significantly in style or structure from those in chapter 3. The only difference is that these final five dates (or more, depending on how many special events you identify) are focused on special occasions that are unique to *you* as individuals and as a couple. Everyone celebrates Valentine's Day, but only the two of you celebrate *your* anniversary. Anyone can enjoy a Christmas date, but only *you* have a unique birthday that you can commemorate with the one you love.

If you're planning to follow the longer list of dates described in chapter 3, make sure you intersperse them, when appropriate, with a few of the special-occasion dates outlined in this chapter. Okay, let's forge ahead.

The Anniversary of Your First Date

*Dating is pressure and tension. What is a date,
really, but a job interview that lasts all night?*
—Jerry Seinfeld, comedian

We didn't technically have a "first date" as you'll read later, but one of
my (Greg's) favorite memories of spending time with Erin before we
were married happened when she helped me move to Denver nine
months before our wedding. The day started out pretty normal. Erin
met me at my parents' house at about 6:00 a.m. We wanted to get an
early start because we had twelve hundred miles to drive from Phoenix
to Denver. By seven o'clock, we had said our good-byes to my family
and figured we could still make Denver by late night. However, trouble was brewing. Around four in the afternoon, I became extremely
tired. I'd been the only one driving up to that point, so I asked Erin
to take over.

"Not on your life," she uttered. "There's no way I'm driving this
big semitruck!" Although I thought she was being rather dramatic,
I understood that I was going to be the only one driving. So I told
her I needed to get some stuff that would keep me awake. We pulled
into a truck stop, and she loaded me up with vitamin B-12, NoDoz
tablets, Jolt Cola, weight-loss pills, basically anything she could find
that contained a high amount of caffeine.

"Are you sure I can take all of this stuff?" I asked, feeling rather
concerned. "Sure. Trust me!" she said. And with that, I overdosed on

caffeine. The moment it hit my system, I felt as if I could drive twelve thousand miles. I smiled at Erin, leaned over, and shouted, "How far is Canada. . . . We're going all the way!"

The thing about caffeine, though, is that it wears off and leaves you feeling like a wet noodle. At one thirty in the morning, I couldn't drive another mile. "If we don't find a place to stop immediately," I whined, "I'm going to kill us." Since we were right outside of Colorado Springs, I figured that would be as good a place as any to stop. However, I quickly discovered how Mary and Joseph must have felt riding into Bethlehem. There wasn't a single room left at the inn! It was parents' weekend at the Air Force Academy. Every lousy room had been rented in every hotel and motel. We searched for an hour before someone finally said, "I guarantee there's a room at this motel downtown." Bingo!

When we arrived at the motel, I pulled the truck around the entire complex. It was U-shaped, with the office shack in the center of the *U*. By this time I was completely exhausted. As a matter of fact, I was almost delirious. "I need two rooms," I said to the office manager.

"I'm afraid I only have one available" was his reply.

"I'll take the one," I finally said after snapping back awake.

"How many hours would you like the room for?" he asked.

What an odd question, I thought. I consulted my watch. *If it's two thirty now, we could sleep for five hours and still make Denver by 9:00 a.m.* So I told him, "I need the room for five hours."

With that, the motel manager smiled and snickered, "Way to go, buddy."

I was so tired that I wasn't following his bantering. "Most of the time," I replied, still confused by his teasing, "I rent a room all night."

And with that he doubled over laughing and gave me a high five. Sadly, it was days later until I realized why he had responded that way. Pervert!

The best part of the trip, however, didn't happen until the next morning. When I went into the office to check out, the same manager was there, and he was quite upset. "Buddy," I inquired, "what's wrong?"

"None of the phones work, and people are yelling at me!" he snapped.

"Tell me about it," I said. "My fiancée and I tried to call our parents to let them know what happened. You see, we didn't want anyone to wonder why we stayed in the same room, so we were going to call our parents and tell them I was going to sleep on the floor, and . . ."

He clearly wasn't interested in my story. So I walked out to buy Erin a Diet Coke from the vending machine and noticed a cable lying on the ground. *That's weird*, I thought. As I walked around the motel complex, every few feet another phone cable was lying on the ground. That is, until you reached my truck. There, six inches from where I had parked, was the last cable, still in place. The instant I realized that I'd taken out all of the phone cables when I drove around the complex the night before, I ran into the room and yelled, "Erin, get into the truck now! We've got to get out of here!" She thought I had just robbed the joint. When it was all said and done, and I had paid for the damage, that cruddy little hourly room ended up costing me a bundle.

Hopefully your first date wasn't filled with such amazing drama. But this brings up an important point. Sometimes those dates early in your relationship were full of pitfalls. There may have been misunderstandings, last-minute changes of plans, and times of sheer awkwardness. After all, you were just getting to know each other, so there were plenty of opportunities for things to go wrong. But don't let that stop you from re-creating them! We still laugh about our crazy misadventures on the trip from Phoenix to Denver. It was rough at the time, but today it's a fun story and an opportunity to laugh, connect, and reminisce.

Also, we should probably state the obvious: Commemorating the anniversary of your first date is something that will appeal more to women than men. There's a decent chance that neither of you remembers the exact calendar day of your first date. But if someone *does* remember, the odds overwhelmingly favor the wife. Women are simply more likely to remember these things, to write them down, and to mention them in casual conversation.

Picture the scene: A married couple is driving around town, simply running errands or heading home from the store. Suddenly the wife exclaims, "Honey! I just realized that twelve years ago, on this very night, we had our first date! Can you believe it? How time flies!" She puts her hand on her husband's knee and smiles wistfully.

Meanwhile, the husband, in a state of utter shock and confusion, can only blurt, "Uh, *of course* it's the twelfth anniversary of our first date! I was just going to mention that fact. Oh, what wonderful memories I have of that night. What did we do again?"

On the other hand, some of you may not even have had a distinct first-date experience. That's certainly true of us. Our relationship grew and flourished within the context of platonic friendship rather than through a formal dating scenario. In fact, our decision to start dating—to take our relationship to the next level—came on a cruise ship! Don't worry, there's nothing salacious to report. I (Greg) was on the cruise with my mom and dad, and Erin was employed as a nanny for another couple on the ship. It was during the cruise that Erin and I articulated our feelings for each other and agreed to pursue a romantic relationship. Shades of *The Love Boat*!

In any event, assuming you did begin dating in more conventional terms, it might not be that important to you to trace your first date back to a specific day on the calendar. Whether you can pinpoint that actual anniversary of your first date or not, you can certainly take steps to *re-create* it. We discussed the idea of re-creating a date in the previous chapter (date 34, "Remembering Again"). That date involved reliving one of your *favorite* or most memorable dates. This date is a bit more specific. If your very first date truly wasn't that noteworthy or, in the case of some couples, was an unmitigated disaster, don't sweat it. Re-create it anyway and redeem the time!

As we mentioned earlier, re-creating dates is a great tool for fostering intimacy because it involves *reminiscing* with your spouse about past good times together. It also helps reawaken those feelings of young love—the anticipation, the rush of excitement, the butterflies in the stomach—and floods your brain with dopamine and norepinephrine, re-creating the sensations you experienced when you first "fell" for each other.

Activity: Whether you're reenacting your very first date or when you got engaged, you likely won't be able to re-create everything down to the last detail. You probably don't even live in the same city where you first met. And even if you do, the romantic restaurant where you had your first rendezvous may have long since closed its doors. Find a suitable alternative that evokes memories of that first date, even if some of the particulars are different. If you saw a movie, find the same film on DVD or online and watch it again at home. If you took pictures on your first date, find any photos and look at them.

Questions: This is a great opportunity to remember, to compare notes, and probably to laugh as well. After your activity, discuss the following questions: Were you nervous before our first date? Do you remember any funny stories? Did anything go wrong on our date—something that seemed utterly catastrophic at the time but that we laugh about now? Were your friends and family members enthusiastic about the prospect of our dating? After that first date, did you have any second thoughts about moving forward? At what point during our dating relationship did you know I was "the one"?

Wedding Anniversary

What greater thing is there for human souls,
than to feel that they are joined for life . . . to be
with each other in silent unspeakable memories.
—George Eliot, *Adam Bede*

As dates go, the anniversary date is probably the biggest no-brainer in the history of no-brainers, with the other possible candidate being the Valentine's Day date (see date 6). Even if you've had a terrible track record for dating since you got married, chances are you've gone out on at least one or two dates to celebrate your wedding anniversary. It's just what most couples do.

Then again, maybe you've never pulled out all the stops to celebrate the day you said "I do" to each other. Perhaps a card or bouquet has sufficed up to this point. Hopefully you haven't been guilty of *forgetting* your anniversary (guys, once again, we're thinking primarily of you here).

Whatever the case, a few hours of uninterrupted couple time is the perfect opportunity to reminisce, to celebrate, to thank God, and to commemorate an event that, along with the births of your children, is among the most momentous occasions of your entire life.

Activity: If you've celebrated your wedding anniversary with a romantic date in the past, don't feel pressured to deviate significantly from that formula now. There's nothing wrong with having a nice candlelight dinner to celebrate your years of wedded bliss. At the same time, if a romantic date is the norm for you on your anniversary, why not try something new this year? Go to a drive-through restaurant and then take your food to the park for a picnic. Try writing each other a love poem. Have T-shirts made commemorating your anniversary and then wear them to the zoo, the local amusement park, or another attraction. In addition, consider the following ideas:

- Get out your wedding photo album or wedding video and relive the memories from your special day.

- Work together on making a new video—with updated photos and clips from your years of marriage—to celebrate your journey together thus far.

- Do any of your groomsmen or bridesmaids still live within driving distance? If so, explore the double-date idea by inviting them and their spouses to join you at a restaurant in celebration of your anniversary. Have fun sharing memories together.

- Consider a night or weekend away to celebrate your anniversary in true uninterrupted style. This is a particularly good option for milestone anniversaries, such as your tenth, fifteenth, twenty-fifth, and so on.

- Don't hesitate to keep it simple. A casual date over coffee and dessert is all it takes for you to have an opportunity to celebrate and remember your wedding day.

Questions: Whether you engage in a full weekend away or a quick visit to a nearby diner, an anniversary date is all about reminiscing. Discuss the following questions: Do you remember any funny stories from our wedding day? Were you stressed? Can you recall anything specific about the pastor's message aside from the standard exchange of vows? What are some of your favorite memories from our honeymoon? If we had the chance to do our wedding or honeymoon again, would we change anything?

Birthday . . . Times Two!

A diplomat is a man who always remembers a
woman's birthday but never remembers her age.
—attributed to Robert Frost

Birthdays are a big deal when you're a kid. You got to invite your friends over for a party involving lots of cake, ice cream, and pin the tail on the donkey. Maybe your mom made cupcakes and brought them to share with all the kids in your class at school. Or perhaps your family went out for dinner at a fun restaurant, where the staff would put on silly hats and sing "Happy Birthday" at your table so that all the other patrons could hear it. By the time you went to bed at night, you were exhausted from all of the fun and from everybody making a fuss over you all day long.

But when you're an adult, birthdays are very different. For one thing, the prospect of being one year older isn't as exciting as it was when you were young. And for another, grown-ups don't really feel the need to make birthdays an event. At the most, your coworkers might put up a couple of birthday balloons in your cubicle and wish you well. Or you might get together for coffee with a friend. And that's it.

If there's anyone who's going to make a big deal of your birthday as an adult—who will fawn over you and make you feel as if you're the most important person in the universe—it should be your spouse! Celebrating your mate's birthday and putting forth a little extra effort to make him or her feel special are great ways to communicate affection and admiration. We know of some spouses who even take a vacation day from work to spend the day with their husbands or wives on their birthdays.

So go ahead, turn your mate's birthday—an occasion many of us dread as we get older—into an opportunity to make him or her feel special, affirmed, and loved!

Activity: There are two approaches you might take when planning a birthday date. The first is to let the birthday girl or boy plan all of the activities. After all, it's *your spouse's* birthday—he or she should be able to choose what to do, right? Another option would be for you to plan the entire date and surprise the birthday boy or girl. There are pros and cons to both of these approaches. Much depends on your own personalities and preferences. If you plan a birthday date *for* your spouse, just make sure you select activities you know he or she will enjoy. If your wife is a private person who appreciates a quiet, romantic evening, you might not want to surprise her with a loud, crowded party featuring fifty of your closest friends. If your husband is an action-movie junkie, don't take him to see *Pride and Prejudice*.

As with any date, the operative word for a birthday date is *fun*. Taking extra care to ensure that your spouse feels like a kid again can be a great way to convey your love for him or her.

Questions: After your activity, be sure to shower your spouse with plenty of love and attention. Look back at some of the dates in chapter 3 that address ways to build intimacy and foster connection by focusing on your mate's unique needs and interests (for example, date 10, "I Cherish You"; date 27, "Touch"; date 28, "Simple Gifts"; and date 40, "Tenderness"). In addition, discuss the following questions: What are some of your favorite birthday memories from childhood? What makes them so special? What is your favorite birthday activity as an adult? Do you dread the idea of having birthdays and getting older? How can I help make sure that birthdays for you are uplifting and fulfilling?

(*Note:* It goes without saying that the birthday date is one you'll want to enjoy at least twice during the year—once for each of your birthdays—so this date actually counts as *two* separate entries in our list of fifty-two dates.)

Milestones

*To get the full value of joy you must
have someone to divide it with.*
—Mark Twain

The final date in our list of fifty-two could actually turn into *several* dates, depending on how many events or milestones you choose to commemorate in this way. Basically, this is a chance for you and your spouse to celebrate any number of significant events in your lives by setting aside some quality couple time together. Some dates happen "just because," and others are tied to certain life developments or special occasions. Either way, the goal is the same: to grow closer to your spouse, to have fun, and to invest in your relationship. There's *always* a good excuse to go on a date!

With that said, here are some life events that you might consider celebrating or commemorating with your spouse.

A Promotion at Work

Activity: Go out for dinner someplace nice, especially if your promotion involved an increase in salary.

Questions: If you got the promotion, be sure to thank your spouse for supporting and encouraging you in achieving this major milestone. If your spouse got the promotion, make an effort to highlight the skills and character traits that likely contributed to him or her being recognized in this way at work.

COMPLETION OF A DEGREE OR
OTHER COURSEWORK

Activity: Whether your classes took place online or on campus, schedule your "graduation date" during the time that normally would have been occupied by your studies. This will drive home the fact that you're *done* with your classes, and that you now have a few extra hours in your week to pursue other activities . . . such as dating your spouse!

Questions: Whether or not you talk specifically about your spouse's degree during your date will depend on your spouse. He or she may take pleasure and pride in sharing with you some of the nuggets of wisdom that were gained while earning the degree. If so, even if the subject in question doesn't particularly light your fire, make sure to show genuine interest and support. On the other hand, after studying for finals and "firing on all cylinders" in that final push before graduation, the *last* thing some students want to do is talk about school! If that's the case for your spouse, make sure your date night is relaxing and fun—a welcome reprieve from talk about economics or theology or business or English.

ACHIEVEMENT OF A PERSONAL
GOAL OR OBJECTIVE

Activity: Perhaps your spouse had a goal of losing twenty pounds or completing a rigorous exercise program. Or maybe he or she has just completed another difficult project—writing a book, building a fence in the backyard, volunteering in a high-risk youth program, or painting the house. Take him or her out on the town to celebrate the achievement!

Questions: This is another chance to show a genuine interest in the things that matter to your spouse. Be sure to offer lots of praise and affirmation and to also ask questions: How do you feel now that you've reached your goal? Would you ever commit to doing something like that again? Do you feel you've grown emotionally or spiritually as a result of completing your task?

COMPLETION OF CHEMOTHERAPY OR ANOTHER INTENSIVE MEDICAL PROCEDURE

Activity: Following a prolonged illness or another physical challenge, going out and feeling "normal" again might just be the thing to brighten your mate's spirits (provided he or she has had adequate time to recover and regain strength, of course). Take your spouse to a nice restaurant or engage in a recreational activity of his or her choosing.

Questions: Although you didn't experience the actual physical symptoms, enduring a serious illness like cancer is certainly something that spouses do *together*. During your date, take time to debrief and talk about how the experience has changed both of you. If your spouse was the one who was ill, make sure to praise him or her for demonstrating strength and resilience in the face of difficult odds. And if you were sick, make every effort to let your spouse know how grateful you are to him or her for walking with you on this journey. End the evening by praying together and giving thanks to God for bringing you and your family through this difficult time. Ask Him to continue drawing you closer to each other and closer to Him through whatever lies ahead—the good and the bad—in your marriage.

Dating Strategies for Engaged Couples

In the last chapter, we mentioned that we really didn't have an official first date. Rather, we were friends for a long time—throughout our college years. We didn't make the decision to start dating until after college, while Erin and I (Greg) were on a cruise. (I was with my parents, and Erin was serving as a nanny for another family.)

Once we started dating, however, things started to progress rapidly . . . until we broke up. It depends on how you look at it! Erin believed that we broke up for a short period, while I was of the opinion that the breakup never actually happened. You see, because we had known each other for so long as friends, we had already built solid relationships with each other's families. As soon as we started dating, my mom and sister started putting big-time pressure on me to pursue the relationship with gusto.

After about a month or so, I started getting nervous. I wasn't having second thoughts about the relationship, but I felt that things were moving too fast, and I wanted to slow down a bit. So I asked Erin out to dinner and basically laid my concerns out on the table. In my mind, I was truly only suggesting that we take the relationship down a notch and not bow to pressure from my family members to forge ahead too fast. But in *Erin's* mind, phrases like *slow down* and *think things through* were simply codes for "Let's call the whole thing off."

By the end of the date, I felt that Erin and I were still dating, albeit more casually, while Erin was under the impression that we had broken up. She mourned the loss of the relationship but was determined to move on. Not long after this, I went out of town with my dad, and Erin went out on dates with several other suitors. When I got back to town and heard from my sister that Erin was dating other people, I almost had a coronary episode!

I called Erin immediately upon hearing this disturbing news. I'm pleased to report that after a lot of conversation and explaining and clarifying on my part, Erin and I were finally back on the same page. We agreed to start dating exclusively, and while we endeavored to take it reasonably slow and not be swayed by the enthusiasm of my mom and sister, it wasn't long before we did, in fact, get engaged.

If you're reading this book as an engaged couple, congratulations on your upcoming nuptials! Hopefully your path to engagement wasn't fraught with the same misunderstandings and drama ours was. Right now, you're likely brimming with enthusiasm, excitement, and the thrill of young love. You're looking forward to your wedding, your honeymoon, and your glorious future together. As you drive around town visiting cake decorators and looking at possible church and reception facilities, you're singing, "The future's so bright, we gotta wear shades."

That's wonderful! We hope you'll never lose that enthusiasm for your relationship and for each other. And honestly, at this point you probably feel you never will. You simply can't imagine yourselves becoming like some of the married couples we've described throughout this book—the ones who have grown apart as a result of the demands of children, careers, and so on. We never thought we would! But after a few kids, we were just like some of those couples.

It doesn't seem possible that your marriage could proceed for months at a time without your going out on a date. Nevertheless, many couples have stood where you stand today, and yet somehow, life became increasingly complicated and complex, leaving them precious little time to invest in each other and foster intimacy in their relationship. Many of the married couples reading this book are having to start from scratch when it comes to investing in their marriage. They're having to rebuild their relationship from the ground up. They may not necessarily have faced a serious problem like adultery or separation; they may simply have let years go by in their marriage when they stopped being intentional about nurturing their relationship because there were too many other things—valid, important things—competing for their attention.

The fact that you're reading this book *before* you marry is a sign that you're committed as a couple not to let that happen in your relationship. One of the messages we've driven home again and again in this book is that married couples have to be *intentional* about fostering intimacy and connection in their relationship. It won't just happen. The good news for *you* is that while many couples don't wake up to this reality until they're five, ten, or twenty years into their marriage, you can make a commitment to do it *right now*, before you've even walked down the aisle or recited your vows.

Here's your chance to start on a solid foundation. By committing to regular date nights throughout your marriage, you'll forge a stronger, deeper relationship that will be better equipped to weather the ups and downs of careers, childrearing, finances, and other real-life issues that threaten to derail couples who aren't connected emotionally, physically, and spiritually. Committing to and being intentional about regular dating *now* is all about establishing a positive, proactive habit that will benefit and enrich you both for the rest of your married lives.

"But wait a minute!" you may be saying. "We already see each other every day now as it is. We're basically going out on a date every single day or night. We realize it won't always be this easy to have uninterrupted couple time, but for now we're doing pretty darn good."

That's a great point. But if you review the preceding chapters, you'll see that spending time together, running errands together, and yes, even planning a wedding together, while all good and necessary pursuits, aren't the same as taking time out of your busy schedules to simply invest in each other and in your relationship. The question to ask yourselves is, "How can we do date nights *better*?" You have more free time and perhaps more disposable income at this point than you're likely to have after five years of marriage. So why not use those resources to invest in dates that are fun and relaxing and that help you strengthen your relationship?

When it comes to dating during engagement, the guidelines are very similar to those we outlined for marital dating in chapter 2. Let's review them again now and consider how they might specifically apply to your situation:

1. *Don't administrate your relationship!* As an engaged couple, this is probably the toughest challenge you'll face as you make a commitment to regular dating. If you're like most couples, two major obstacles will threaten to derail your dates.

The first obstacle is dealing with issues related to your premarital counseling. Now, if you read that sentence and asked, "Wait—what's premarital counseling?" we definitely have a problem. If you're engaged and rapidly heading toward marriage, and you haven't gotten involved in some form of premarital counseling, you need to do so as soon as possible. Some couples resist doing this with the rationale, "We're deliriously happy, and we aren't even married yet. Why on earth would we want to see a counselor?"

But counseling isn't just for troubled couples. We advise every engaged couple to seek premarital counseling, whether they come from rosy, stable backgrounds, or their lives were marred by abuse and addiction prior to the engagement. It simply makes good sense, and it dramatically decreases the chances of encountering serious issues after you've tied the knot. Getting premarital counseling isn't an admission that there's something wrong with your relationship. Rather, it's a commitment on both your parts to do everything possible to make your relationship the best it can possibly be. Without being aware of your strengths and areas that need growth, and without an end in mind, it's difficult to create the marriage you've always dreamed of.

If you're not currently involved in premarital counseling, you can start by taking Focus on the Family's Couple Checkup. We covered this earlier for married couples, but there is also a version of the checkup designed specifically for engaged couples. Just go to *focusonthefamily.com/couplecheckup* and click on the "Engaged" link. You can also contact Focus on the Family at 1-800-A-FAMILY for a referral to a licensed counselor in your area. Alternatively, you might ask the pastor who will be officiating your wedding about the possibility of meeting him for a few premarital-counseling sessions, or inquire at your church about a premarital Sunday school class, small group, or program. We encourage couples to think beyond the wedding day. That's why we wrote the book *Before You Plan Your Wedding . . . Plan Your Marriage.*[1]

Here's the issue with dating, though. Once you're on board with premarital counseling, you need to take steps to ensure that it doesn't derail your date nights! In meeting with your premarital counselor, you'll likely discuss things like your spiritual beliefs, your personality types, conflict, communication, and other issues of importance as you start building your lives together. Your counselor may even give you a workbook or other material to study together. This is very important, and you should certainly set aside time to do it—*but not on your date nights* (or afternoons or mornings). As we have stressed repeatedly throughout this book, your dates are for having fun and fostering relational intimacy with your fiancé(e). So make sure your date nights are fun, relaxed, and conflict-free, and save the more serious (but equally important) premarital-counseling material for another time.

In addition to premarital counseling, another administrative activity will dominate your date nights if you allow it to. Can you guess what it is? That's right—*wedding plans*! In fact, it's safe to say that once the engagement becomes official, wedding plans tend to overshadow just about every other aspect of most engaged couples' relationships. From finding bridesmaids' dresses to reserving a church and reception facility to getting fitted for a tuxedo to selecting flowers and fabrics to planning the rehearsal dinner to buying gifts for the groomsmen to selecting a wedding cake to sending out invitations to making honeymoon plans to a thousand other responsibilities, planning the wedding can completely consume a young couple in love (not to mention put a significant strain on their relationship!).

Early on, this kind of activity might seem "fun" (especially to the bride-to-be) and therefore like a good candidate for a date-night activity. However, more often than not, chasing down all the minute details necessary to pull off a wedding becomes tedious and tiresome—definitely more of an administrative activity than a fun activity.

For this reason, we suggest, once again, that you not allow the tyranny of wedding plans to intrude on your date nights. Yes, you should certainly devote time—often "together time"—to planning the ceremony and other details. But make every effort to separate that from your dates. Your dates should be opportunities to connect, relax, and unwind. Resist the urge to let the details of the ceremony intrude on your scheduled couple time. Among other things, this means that while you're on a date, you shouldn't be using your iPhone to answer emails from the caterer or on Facebook with your groomsmen about the bachelor-party plans. Save those conversations for later!

2. *Stay current.* There's a big difference between knowing someone well—well enough to make a lifelong commitment to that person in marriage—and knowing absolutely *everything* there is to know about that person. The first is an important goal for engaged couples; the second is quite simply impossible for anyone and everyone.

When we talked about staying current earlier in the book, the idea is that spouses need to be *students* of each other. Why? Because there's always something new to learn. You can never have someone totally figured out or know everything there is to know about that person, even if that person is your spouse or fiancé(e).

Regular dates afford you the opportunity to stay curious about each other, to update your information about one another, and to keep up to speed on your fiancé(e)'s ever-changing desires, tastes, preferences, and personality. It's important to make staying current with your future mate a habit and priority now, so that you can carry that mind-set into your marriage. As we said in chapter 1, you don't want to wake up next to your husband or wife twenty years from now and realize that you're strangers living under the same roof!

3. *Try new and exciting activities.* In a certain sense, everything you do as an engaged couple may seem new and exciting. Even routine activities take on an added significance once you've made that momentous decision to commit yourselves to another person for the rest of your lives. As we mentioned earlier, when you experience new activities and events together, your brains are producing dopamine and norepinephrine—neurotransmitters that contribute significantly to the "high" of falling in love.

This all sounds very clinical and unromantic, but the fact is that trying new activities can strengthen your bond with each other. Even though the excitement of getting engaged permeates your relationship, do you ever feel as if things have grown a bit stale? Do you still get the same feelings of elation when you're together now that you did when you first laid eyes on each other across a crowded room? If not, adding some variety to your date nights can reinvigorate some of those feelings of young love. As we said in chapter 2, the keys are *novelty* and *fun*.

4. *Reminisce.* Reminiscing about good times is especially important for long-married couples because it helps strengthen their relationship through the bond of past shared experiences. As they reflect on enjoyable times in the past, it fills them with anticipation of more good times in the future.

As a newly engaged couple, you obviously don't have twenty years of shared experiences from which to draw when you sit down to reminisce. But reminiscing isn't only an activity for gray-haired people in rocking chairs. If you're like us, you probably have a deep pool of good memories together from the months or years before you got engaged. As you may recall, we were good friends throughout college, and although we didn't start dating until after we graduated, we still had several years' worth of friendship memories accumulated by the time we got engaged. Be sure your engagement-period dates are filled with fun memories about the time you first met, your first date, funny or heartwarming stories from your relationship thus far, and so on.

Here's one of our favorites: Soon after Erin and I (Greg) agreed to start dating, we served as camp counselors at a large Christian sports camp in Branson, Missouri. I wanted to make the most of this new phase of our relationship, so I knew that I needed to do something other than dinner and movie. My first mistake was that I didn't ask any females for their opinions on how I could impress Erin. Instead, I consulted my fellow male counselors for guidance.

The advice I received was to take Erin on a picnic down by the lake, and then for a swim. That might sound okay, but no. After twenty-one years of marriage, I now understand that a dating relationship shouldn't begin by forcing the girl into a bathing suit. The only way that sounds right is if you're a hormonal, college kid. Which I actually was!

Anyway, Erin and I actually had a great picnic, and then we decided to go for a swim in the lake. Unfortunately, the water was freezing! Lake Taneycomo averages forty-eight degrees, so we weren't even able to wear regular bathing suits. We put on full-length scuba suits and braved the icy water.

As we were having fun swimming around, we noticed some kids hanging out on the dock. We realized that they couldn't see us because we were wearing our dark wet suits. So we decided to have a little bit of fun. Actually, Erin devised the most devilish of plans. We stayed close to the shore and waded through the reeds. By this time, the kids were sitting on the dock with their feet dangling over the side. We slithered quietly under the dock, undetected.

Now most youth camps have their share of traditional scary stories and legends, and this one was no exception. We used to tell the kids frightening tales about the Slew Lady—a woman who was killed in the camp pond that we called the Slew. She went on to haunt the camp and would go after kids who went swimming in the lake. As a result of these scary stories perpetuated by the camp counselors, most of the younger kids would never swim. Instead, they would just sit on the dock, keeping out a watchful eye for the Slew Lady.

Back under the dock, we prepared for the Slew Lady's grand entrance. Erin used her fingers and mouthed the words "One . . . two . . . three!" and then she sprang out from under the dock and lunged at the poor boys who were already too afraid to go into the water. At the same time I screamed, "Watch out! It's the Slew Lady!"

The result of Erin's joke was total pandemonium. Most of the boys' high-pitched screams reached levels that only a few species of animals were able to hear. They scattered in every direction and never looked back. However, if they could have gotten a glimpse under the dock, they would have seen a female counselor embracing a male counselor—foreshadowing amazing things to come!

You likely have fun memories like this from the early days of your relationship. So reminisce about them and celebrate them!

5. *Select dating activities that communicate intimacy to both of you.* *Intimacy* can be a terrifying and uncomfortable term for engaged couples—especially for those who embrace a biblical worldview and are therefore committed to remaining sexually pure until their wedding night. We certainly hope you and your fiancé(e) have safeguards in

place to ensure that you don't find yourselves in compromising situations or in the path of unbearable temptation before your wedding.

But there are many levels of intimacy, and when it comes to engaged couples, the type we have in mind isn't of the sexual variety. You may recall that in chapter 2 we cited the Dictionary.com definition of *intimacy* as "a close, familiar, and usually affectionate or loving relationship with another person." As an engaged couple, it's important for you to pursue a close, familiar, and yes, even affectionate (although not sexual) relationship with each other. We actually like the definition of *intimacy* as "into-me-see"! It's really one of the deepest human desires of the *heart*—to be known, loved, and fully accepted.

But as we noted in chapter 2, even when sex is taken out of the equation, men and women define *intimacy* in very different ways. For a man, the simple act of engaging in an activity with a woman—going out for coffee, playing miniature golf, seeing a movie—is enough to communicate intimacy. In the man's mind, the very act of engaging in one of these activities *together* signifies that he and his partner are intimate.

For women, however, the activity itself is only a backdrop to what is really needed to achieve an intimate connection: *good conversation*. For the woman, going out for coffee or going bowling isn't enough if it isn't accompanied by the opportunity to converse at a deep level. Through conversation, she feels connected. I (Greg) can think of a million times when Erin has just wanted to verbally emote—this makes her feel close to me. Our favorite time to do this is when we take walks together. It gives us the opportunity to talk and stay connected. When we were engaged, we would sometimes go to the park and shoot baskets and talk!

So remember, for both you and your fiancé(e) to feel you've made an intimate connection on a date, the date must include *both* a fun activity and the opportunity for meaningful conversation. Some dates may have a slightly heavier emphasis on one over the other, but overall, a fun activity and great conversation should play a part in the proceedings.

Now that we've reviewed the guidelines for successful dating, feel free to go back to chapter 3 and make some of the date-night ideas for married couples your own. There are a few you should consider off-limits for obvious reasons. "Passion" (date 9) and "Touch" (date 27), for example, contain a decidedly sexual component, and as such should be reserved for after marriage. The same goes for "The Weekend Getaway" (date 24). In other words, feel free to disregard any information you feel could lead you astray or entice you into areas of physical contact or conversation that go against the safeguards you've put in place for your relationship.

That being said, there are plenty of dates you'll find incredibly fulfilling and enjoyable as an engaged couple. Here are five examples:

1. *"Windshield Time!"* (date 8)—You already spend a great deal of time in the car together (if nothing else, racing back and forth between the caterer, the florist, the premarital-counselor's office, and other wedding-planning activities). How do you use your time together in the car? Are you simply trying to get from point A to point B? Or are you using the time to foster intimacy and deepen your knowledge of each other? Learning to maximize windshield time is a skill that will benefit you not only for the remainder of your engagement but throughout your married life.

2. *"I Cherish You"* (date 10)—What do you cherish about your fiancé(e)? How would you communicate those feelings to him or her? Create a cherish list for each other and then carry those lists around throughout these busy days of engagement as a means of reaffirming your love and care for one another.

3. *"Laugh with Me"* (date 14)—Laughter is good for the soul, and it's also good for your relationship! Scientists have documented the numerous physical, emotional, spiritual, and psychological benefits of laughter and humor. Engage in a date activity that will enable you to laugh together as a couple.

4. *"Double-Date!"* (date 29)—Couple time is important, but there's also great benefit in investing in others' lives and allowing them to invest in yours. This is true in marriage, and it's true during this period of engagement. Go out on a date with another couple and get to know them better. This could be another engaged couple (resist the temptation to talk exclusively about your respective wedding plans), another couple (perhaps younger) who is only casually dating and with whom you could perhaps share from the wisdom of your limited experience, or an older, married couple who might have a few insights of their own to share with you.

Actually, whether you're engaged or already married, the concept of double dating is too vast and complex a subject to be confined to only one point or one date. So we're going to devote the final chapter of this book to the concept of double dating in all of its glorious manifestations and configurations. While the chapter is written primarily with married couples in mind, we believe you'll find a great deal of relevant, useful information for engaged couples as well.

5. *"Connect"* (date 30)—If you're in your twenties or thirties, you likely have a firm grasp of the wide range of personal technologies and social media available today—iPhones, iPads, Twitter, Facebook, and so on. While these conveniences are useful, there's no denying that they can turn into distractions and even obsessions that hinder our ability to connect with people in the real world. Engage in a date that enables you to practice wisely using these technologies and social-networking formats to connect with each other in meaningful, proactive ways during those times when you're apart, both during your engagement and after you marry.

The Power of Double Dating

Before putting this book to bed and launching you, dear readers, on a lifelong journey of fun marital dates, we thought it might be helpful to further explore a subject that has come up several times throughout the book: *double dating*.

Some of our best dates have happened because we called up a couple of friends and asked if they wanted to go on an impromptu double date. One of the most memorable of those double dates happened when we lived in northwest Arkansas. A couple we love hanging out with dropped by, and we decided to go out for a quick dinner. We laughed and enjoyed great conversation together.

This particular double date took place during the winter, so it was really cold outside. On the drive back to our house after dinner, I (Greg) could have sworn that I kept hearing a very strange noise. At one point I even shushed everyone in the car so we could listen as a group. And sure enough, Erin and the other couple could hear the noise as well. We just couldn't figure out what it was! It sounded almost like an animal shrieking. It was very creepy!

When we pulled into our garage and got out of the van, the four of us were met with the most awful sound. Something was screaming out in pain. You know how the Bible talks about "weeping and gnash-ing of teeth" (Matthew 8:12)? That's what it sounded like.

The women screamed and ran inside the house. My friend and I stood there, paralyzed with fear. What type of ferocious monster could be hiding in our garage? Eventually we realized that the screams were emanating from under the car. Maybe we had run over the evil beast? We got down on our hands and knees and cautiously looked around. But we couldn't find the source of the demented howling. We searched and searched and finally concluded that "it" could be in only one place—under the hood.

I unlatched the hood, and together we slowly raised it. The hood was only about halfway open when total chaos ensued. All I remem-ber seeing was a little black ball of fur jumping right at us. We both screamed and dropped the hood. It took us several seconds to compre-hend what we were staring at. In the corner of the garage, the savage creature turned out to be a little black cat.

Our best guess as to how this poor kitten had gotten trapped under our hood was that while we were at the restaurant, it had climbed up inside the engine to escape the cold. It must have been warming itself on the van's warm engine block when we drove off. The strange noise we heard while driving home must have been the cat screaming for help. And who could blame it? I would have screamed for help too, if I was stuck in a running car engine!

We tried to help the cat, which was now hissing at us in the corner of the garage, with every last hair standing straight up. But as we came close, the poor creature took off like a rocket. I'm certain that it will think twice before warming itself on another engine block.

This experience was no picnic for the traumatized cat, but it sure makes for a good story that we can share and laugh about with the other couple we double-dated with that night.

We've formed deeper relationships with several couples through double dating over the years. In fact, for our fifteenth wedding anniversary, we took a trip to Hawaii with two other couples with whom we had enjoyed double dates throughout our time in grad school many years ago. Those relationships are so important to us!

Now, it's certainly true that the majority of your dates should be devoted to one-on-one couple time. We've already established that modern family life is exceedingly busy and demanding, and for that reason alone, it's critical that you set aside time for yourselves to relax, have fun, and invest in your relationship.

At the same time, the concept of living in community, of sharing your life and experiences with others, is very important. Your marriage isn't an island. On occasion, you need the chance to interact with other couples—to invest in their lives and allow them to invest in yours. This is especially important in our day and age when the typical family unit is far removed from the influence of grandparents, aunts, uncles, and other extended-family members. Without that network of support, you need to have the influence of good friends and acquaintances in your lives.

During troubled times, the Evil One likes nothing more than to isolate couples, causing them to believe that they are the only ones to experience challenges and hardships in their relationship. Building strong friendships with other couples allows you to have someone else to talk to not only during the painful times in your marriage but during the joyous times as well. We were created for community!

As followers of Christ, it's also important for us to interact and be connected with other believers. There's a special bond between brothers and sisters in Christ. It's important to have people in your life who can speak truth to you and can come alongside you in both good and bad times. This is at least partly what Paul had in mind when he wrote to the church at Thessalonica, "Therefore encourage one another and build each other up, just as in fact you are doing" (1 Thessalonians 5:11).

With these thoughts in mind, we encourage you to devote at least a few dates a year to double dates with other couples in your circle of influence. There's no hard-and-fast rule, of course, but perhaps you could set a goal of making one out of every four dates a double date. If you're on the ambitious once-a-week dating schedule, that would mean you have a double date once a month. If scheduling and budgetary considerations limit you to only one date per month, you'll still be able to squeeze in three double dates over the course of a year.

Once you've determined to make double dating part of your schedule, the question then becomes, "Who should we ask out?" In several ways, this process can mirror what single men and women experience when they're preparing to go out on a date for the first time. "Will he like me?" "Will our interests and beliefs align?" "Will she think I'm cool?" "I want to make a good impression!" Funny as it may seem, as a couple you might ask yourselves some of these same types of questions as you consider asking out a new couple for the first time!

This brings up an important point. Don't limit your double-date choices to only those couples whom you know extremely well and whom you already consider great friends. There's certainly nothing wrong with double dating with your close friends, but many other couples out there could enrich your lives and stretch your boundaries. Yes, even after you're married, it can be fun meeting *new* people!

Think about it. At some point you've probably encountered a couple in your church, or from work, whom you'd like to get to know better. You may have seen one another in passing and said, "We should hang out sometime." But months passed and it never happened. Then finally, maybe at a church picnic or an office party, you finally had a chance to spend some quality time with this other couple—and you loved it! Everyone in your group clicked. The wives discovered a shared love of Pinterest, and the guys had a blast discussing the finer points of collecting vintage vinyl albums by U2. Plus, you also discovered that both couples share a love of camping. Suddenly you found yourselves asking, "Why did it take us so long to get together?" That's what can happen when you take the chance to reach out and engage with another couple! Within the course of one evening, you went from being casual acquaintances to good friends.

At the same time, as you consider which couples might make good candidates for a double date, don't feel the pressure of becoming BFFs (best friends forever) with *every* couple you hang out with. You haven't failed if by the end of the evening, you don't feel the urge to write the other couple into your will or make them the godparents of your children. Some relationships take longer to deepen and develop, and others never make it past the surface stage. That's okay!

Sometimes it takes only one double date to realize that you aren't going to click with another couple, and that you may, in fact, feel awkward around one another. (Again, isn't it interesting how this mirrors the dating experiences of single men and women?) Don't worry if every double date doesn't leave you feeling wowed. Even if you see certain couples only once and then move on, there's no reason those experiences can't be fulfilling and enlightening in their own way. You may not make a strong connection with that other couple, but going through the experience together can help deepen your own relationship as a couple.

At the end of the day, friendships and relationships with other couples are good for you and for your marriage. There's something special about sitting across the table from another couple over a satisfying meal and sharing your stories, your experiences, and your lives. It isn't the same thing as a girls' night out for the wife or a guys' night out for the husband (although those events are important on occasion too). As we said earlier, double dating enables you, as a couple, to invest in the lives of another couple and opens the door for that couple to make the same investment in you. That's what fellowship is all about.

Three Stages of Life

One of the exciting things about double dating is that it allows you the opportunity to connect with couples of various ages in different stages of life. We have broken them down into three separate categories. Let's consider, for a moment, how each age group or life stage might impact your double-dating activities.

Younger Couples

If you're reading this book as a newlywed couple in your early twenties, you'll probably have to search long and hard before you can find a *younger* couple with whom you can engage in a double date. However, if you have even two or three years of marriage under your belts, the playing field increases significantly. There's likely a newlywed couple nearby—in your church or at work, or even a married cousin or extended-family member—who would enjoy spending time with a couple like you, who is just a few years into the marital journey. In fact, the chances are that a newlywed couple would relish the opportunity to spend time with a couple who has genuine marriage experience and yet isn't significantly older. This can help the younger couple feel as if they're dealing more or less with a couple who is their equal rather than one that's old enough to be their parents.

Peer Couples

Assuming that the majority of our readers are couples who are engaged in building careers, childrearing, and so on, a peer couple would be in that same general stage of life. This could include close friends as well as casual acquaintances from church, small group, work, neighborhood, or your kids' school. Because you're in the same stage of life, these couples are likely the easiest to connect with and relate to. Whether you double-date with close friends or relative strangers, there should be no shortage of conversation topics to discuss: the challenges of career; the joys and challenges of raising kids; common interests in music, movies, books, and recreation; and perhaps shared spiritual beliefs.

On that last point, though, don't feel that you have to limit your double dates to couples who share your faith and worldview. It's okay to have fun with a couple who comes from a Hindu background, or who is agnostic (as long as you don't engage in activities with them that violate your faith principles or theirs). Even with different religious backgrounds, you likely have much in common. As the relationship develops and deepens, God may even open up the door for you to share your faith. But don't make evangelizing your main motivation for double dating a couple from a different faith tradition (or none at all). No one wants to go out with a couple who only sees them as a "project"—a mission field to be conquered. Certainly we should always be open to the possibility of sharing our faith as the Holy Spirit leads. But that's the point: Make sure you allow the Holy Spirit to lead. Don't consider your double dates with couples from a different faith background a failure if they never express an interest in Christianity, or even if they seem resistant. It may be that God simply wants you to set an example and "plant a seed," as it were, by your lifestyle. He may have another individual or couple in mind, even years down the road, to reap the harvest. Don't feel pressure to "close the deal" when you're spending time with a non-Christian couple. That's the Holy Spirit's work, and you should endeavor to trust Him to know what to say and when to say it. In the meantime, follow the example of St. Francis of Assisi, who said, "Let all [believers] . . . preach by their deeds."

Older Couples

You might think it a strange idea to consider going out on a double date with an older couple, but there are many benefits to doing this, and you might just be surprised at how many older couples would relish the opportunity to hang out with some young whippersnappers like you! By "older," we mean anything from a couple who has been married just a few years longer than you to a husband and wife who long ago celebrated their fiftieth wedding anniversary. In essence, an older couple will not only be older but will have more life experience than you. It's just a matter of how *much* more. It could be a few years, or it could be several decades.

We have double-dated with couples from each stage of life. It's a joy to connect with couples from all seasons of life, having dinner at our house or theirs, going out to dinner, seeing a movie, or engaging in another fun activity together. The one requirement for any double date is *laughter*!

One thing to think about when considering a double date with an older couple is the subject of *mentoring*. Several authors, most notably Drs. Les and Leslie Parrott, have written extensively about the benefits of marriage mentoring. Sadly, many young couples today come from broken homes and environments in which strong, committed marriages weren't the norm. They have never had a loving, thriving marriage modeled for them, and as a result, they enter into their own marriages with no real clue as to how to proceed. Marriage mentors can be a wellspring of advice, counsel, and insight for couples in this situation, as well as simply good role models.

But marriage mentors aren't just for couples who come from troubled backgrounds or childhoods. *Everyone* who is married can benefit from the wisdom, the experience, and the example of an older, more seasoned couple. Again, Drs. Les and Leslie Parrott have written a great deal on this important subject. Here's a brief list of topics and roles the Parrotts have outlined for marriage mentors:

Preparing: Mentoring Engaged and Newlywed Couples
- Establishing marital roles and responsibilities
- Managing conflict
- Handling money
- Enjoying physical intimacy
- Dealing with the in-laws
- Celebrating holidays and creating family traditions
- Developing the honeymoon habit

Maximizing: Mentoring Couples from Good to Great
- Moving from plodding to purpose
- The need for love talk (communication)
- Moving from selfishness to service
- Parenting with pleasure
- The role of humor and laughter

Repairing: Mentoring Couples in Distress
- Battling addictions
- Surviving infidelity
- Coping with infertility
- Dealing with loss[1]

"Yikes!" you're probably saying. "Those things sound an awful lot like 'administrating' our dates, and that's a no-no, even for double dates, isn't it?" You're absolutely right. And that's why it's important to note that as you consider double dating with an older couple, establishing a formal, official mentoring relationship should *not* be your first priority. The best marriage mentoring happens only after the younger and older couples have built a relationship, established trust, and here it is again, had *fun* together. Approaching an older couple sight unseen and asking them to mentor you—a process that is often intense and intimate—could work in theory, but mentoring is so much more likely to be successful when it happens naturally, out of an established relationship built on trust and familiarity. During our first year of marriage, our dear friends Gary and Carrie Oliver poured into our marriage in this way, and it was a tremendous boost to our relationship.

Oh, and a word of clarification is in order here. In the section on peer couples, we mentioned that it isn't necessary to always double-date with couples who share your faith and Christian worldview. That's true of older couples, too, *unless* you're hoping that the relationship will evolve and eventually progress to mentoring. If you're going to be mentored by an older couple, it's important that they share your basic beliefs and values. If there's a strong disconnect in this area, neither the mentor couple nor the couple being mentored is likely to find the relationship very satisfying.

So, by all means, ask out an older couple and be open to the idea of an official mentoring relationship later down the line. In the meantime, though, just have fun interacting with a couple who is in a different stage of life and who has stood where you now stand. You'll likely learn a lot simply by osmosis as you engage in fun and stimulating activities with them. And guess what? They'll learn from you as well. As the Parrotts point out, relationships of this nature involve a "boomerang effect" in which older couples who invest in younger couples often end up receiving as much as they give.[2] So go out, have fun, and don't feel pressure to commit to a more formal mentoring relationship until both parties have expressed a willingness and interest in doing so.

In case you're wondering, these three double-dating categories (younger couples, peer couples, and older couples) are loosely based on what some Christian teachers have called the Paul-Barnabas-Timothy Principle. The idea is that each of us needs an older person in our lives whom we can look up to and learn from (as Timothy looked up to Paul, so you can learn from an older couple), a peer to encourage us (as Barnabas partnered with Paul, so you can partner with peer couples in your circle of influence), and a younger person we can encourage and to whom we can pass along wisdom (as Paul shared his wisdom and experience with Timothy, so you can invest in a younger couple).

But just remember, all of this talk about mentoring and investing doesn't change the fact that, ultimately, your double dates need to be *fun*. If you'll make having fun and building relationships your priority, the learning, mentoring, and influencing will take care of themselves.

The Nuts and Bolts of Double Dating

As with the other types of dates described in this book, there are a few things you should keep in mind before embarking on a double date. As with a regular date, a double date isn't the time to administrate. This will likely not be a huge challenge on a double date, as few couples will feel tempted to administrate their own marriage while in the presence of another couple.

However, a variation on the administrate theme may present itself when you're out with a peer couple. If you're in the throes of childrearing, and you're out with another couple in the same stage of life, what usually happens? That's right—you spend the entire time talking about *your kids*. You tell funny stories about the cute things they've done. You describe the frustrations of having too many extracurricular activities and of grappling with unruly behavior. Now, we're not saying that talking about your kids should be totally off-limits during a double date. For one thing, many stay-at-home moms can feel very isolated at times, and having the opportunity to discuss their joys and sorrows with other moms can be extremely therapeutic and freeing. So go ahead and make the kids a topic of conversation on your double date—but just make sure it's not the *only* topic.

Allow time to talk about other aspects of your lives and your marital relationships.

And, just as with other dates, do all of this within the context of a fun, shared activity. Just as doing new and exciting things can help deepen your connection as a couple, so doing those same things can strengthen the bonds of friendship between you and the couples with whom you enjoy double dating. And depending on your history with the couple in question, you may be able to engage in the act of *reminiscing* as well. Talk about past double dates you've enjoyed, or other activities you've experienced together.

Oh, and whether you know the couple well or have just met, make sure to put your double date on the calendar. It may feel awkward at first, being so intentional and structured about a time that's supposed to be all about fun, but as we've already established, if you don't set aside a specific time for date nights on your schedule, they likely won't happen. So make sure you and the other couple have the time set aside as far in advance as possible. Looking forward to a double date and counting down the days on the calendar is half the fun!

Okay, we've covered quite a bit of ground already. But before we put a bow on this chapter, we'd like to present a few activities and topics of conversation you might incorporate into your double dating. In addition, make sure to review the material on double dating in chapter 3 (date 29, "Double-Date"), and consider whether some of the other dates in that chapter might be adapted into a double-date format. Certainly many of the suggested activities in chapter 3 could be incorporated into a double date. Some of the questions and conversation topics, however, are better suited for a more intimate setting between just you and your spouse.

Double-Dating Activities

Following are nine ideas for double dates that may appeal to you:

1. *A ball game.* If you think about it, a warm summer evening at a baseball game might be the perfect double-date activity. There's enough going on down on the baseball diamond that you don't have to feel pressure to fill the entire evening with conversation. At the same time, if you and the other couple *do* have a lot to talk about, it's perfectly acceptable to ignore the game altogether and just chat. You won't be disturbing your fellow patrons in the same way you would be if you started talking in the middle of a movie or a ballet.

2. *Miniature golf.* This activity came up a few times in chapter 3, but it's worth attempting as a double date, too. Depending on your moods and preferences, you could play couple against couple or guys against girls or just have a good old-fashioned, four-way competition for the title of Miniature Golf Champion. You can employ the same approach with bowling and other low-impact sports.

3. *Darts.* Playing darts has made a bit of a comeback in recent years. Some restaurants offer free access to dartboards for their patrons. Assuming you can find a venue that isn't overly loud or obnoxious, this could be a great way to connect with another couple. Playing darts could serve as your fun activity (and again, you can divide into teams, if you wish), and you'd also have access to plenty of food and drink for when you're ready to just sit across the table from one another and converse. If darts isn't your thing, you can probably find an establishment that offers pool, air hockey, or a similar game.

4. *Cooking together.* This activity comes in handy when you're double-dating with a peer couple and childcare isn't available. Bring the kids over, set them up in the basement with an assortment of

toys and games, and then spend the evening creating a culinary masterpiece in the kitchen with the other couple. This affords you the opportunity of trying something new (make sure you find an exotic recipe!) and also enables you to practice working as a team. Do too many cooks spoil the broth? Not if you work together!

5. *A service project.* You may have attempted a service project as a couple, but an activity of this nature is definitely something for which there is strength in numbers. Look for volunteer opportunities in your community and then turn that service opportunity into a double date. Or create your own good deed that you and another couple could accomplish together. This is a great way for couples to interact and share insights into the types of activities they feel passionate about (e.g., mercy ministry, homeless outreach, missions, nursing-home outreach).

6. *Shared interests.* In chapter 3 we outlined a date designed to help you and your spouse foster common interests (date 7, "Shared Interests"). Do you share a love of history? Do you enjoy hiking? Invite another couple to enjoy that activity with you and then be open to the possibility of engaging in an activity they enjoy. Have fun expanding one another's horizons.

7. *Karaoke.* We also shared this as a solo-couple date idea, but karaoke is one of those activities that only gets more fun (and more funny!) as you add participants. So find another couple and head to a karaoke bar. Have fun belting out the greatest hits of Journey and Def Leppard and be prepared to cut loose and laugh! If you're uncomfortable with the idea of frequenting a karaoke bar, chip in together on a home karaoke machine. Or perhaps you have Rock Band or a similar game on your family's Wii or Xbox system. This is a relatively

inexpensive way for couples to channel their inner rock star in the comfort of their own homes.

8. *A tour group.* There are likely fun attractions in your own area that you haven't explored before. You'd be surprised how many people right here in Colorado Springs have never visited the top of Pikes Peak, for example. Visiting some local attractions with another couple is a great way to build friendship while experiencing the wonders of the world around you. And if time and budget allow, remember that the world is much bigger than your own hometown. We once traveled to Italy with a group and spent a lot of time sightseeing and diving with two couples, in particular.

9. *Camping.* This activity requires more of a time commitment, and may also necessitate the involvement of your kids (unless both couples can somehow procure overnight childcare). It's probably not the sort of activity you'd want to attempt with a couple you don't know very well. However, under the right conditions, this can be a great way to deepen your friendship with another couple. It will afford you the opportunity to have deeper conversations than you would have during a regular double date, to pray together, and so on. What could be more bonding than living off the land and eking out your existence in the great outdoors?

We've shared nine brief ideas with you, and yet we've only scratched the surface. By applying a little creativity, you should have no trouble coming up with some additional fun, interactive, and new activities for those times when you engage in double dates. And the good news is, you don't have to come up with all of the activities on your own. The other couple likely has their own ideas for fun double-date activities. So put your heads together!

Double-Dating Topics for Discussion

Obviously, the topics of conversation on your double dates will depend on a number of factors, including how well you know the other couple and what stage of life each couple is in. Nevertheless, here is a list of six potential topics you might explore on various double dates:

1. *Introductory information.* Obviously, this is the type of conversation you might pursue with a couple you haven't spent time with previously. The usual conversation-starter topics work well for this type of double date: What do you do for a living? Where do you work? Describe a typical day in your life. Tell us about your kids. Are you doing what you thought you'd be doing at this stage of your life? What are some of your hobbies and interests?

2. *Digging deeper.* Once you grow more familiar with a particular couple, you'll want to learn more about them. You might want to take turns telling your "story"—how and where you met your spouse, what your dating or courtship was like, funny anecdotes from your wedding and honeymoon, and so on. Additional questions might include, "What were your childhoods like?" "Tell us about your families of origin."

3. *Spirituality.* If the couple you're double dating shares your faith, then you already share a bond that goes deeper than what many friends experience. If everyone feels comfortable doing so, take turns sharing your personal testimonies. Talk about what God is doing in your lives. Talk about your church experiences, but try to focus on the positive rather than bashing the churches and/or leaders who have let you down. Ask, "How can we pray for you?" If the couple you're with doesn't share your faith, that doesn't mean spirituality has to be totally off-limits. You don't want to preach at them, but you also shouldn't

feel the need to hide the fact that you're Christians, that you attend church, and so forth. Use discernment.

4. *Exchanging advice.* The more you get to know another couple, the easier it is to invest in their lives and to allow them to invest in yours. Perhaps you're struggling with an issue at work that you could discuss with the other couple. Or maybe the other couple is experiencing in-law troubles, and you can offer a friendly word of advice or caution because you've experienced something similar. This doesn't mean your dates should turn into negative venting sessions. You still need to have some lighthearted fun. But there's nothing wrong with broaching more serious topics as they come up in the course of conversation. That's what friends are for.

5. *Parenting.* We noted earlier in the chapter that for couples who are immersed in the childrearing years, it can be tempting to fill every date and every conversation with talk about their kids. If you allow this to happen, you will likely find your double dates less fulfilling and enriching. You may come to the end of the evening and realize that you know everything there is to know about the other couple's *children*, but you learned very little about the couple themselves. Even so, while you shouldn't let talk about your kids dominate your date, there's certainly nothing wrong with sharing stories, anecdotes, and even advice about childrearing when appropriate. After all, raising kids is a major part of your lives, and it would be unnatural to suppress talking about it altogether. Just try to keep the kid talk in balance.

6. *Hopes and dreams.* The better you get to know certain couples, the more comfortable you'll feel sharing your hopes and dreams with them. As your friendship grows, you'll likely find yourselves asking questions like "Where do you hope to be in your career ten years from

now? Fifteen years?" "What goals do you have for your marriage in the years ahead?" "What are your retirement plans?" "Is there anything significant you'd like to achieve before you die?"

Again, these suggested conversation topics and questions are only a drop in the bucket compared to the vast ocean of stimulating conversation and relationship building that await you as you make a commitment to going on an occasional double date.

Speaking of which, you may be feeling a little overwhelmed at the thought of identifying couples in different stages of life to ask out on dates. Eventually it would be rewarding for you if you could find at least one couple in each category (younger couple, peer couple, older couple) to ask on a double date. But don't worry about that right now. Our challenge to you at this point is to simply ask *one couple*, of any age or in any stage of life, out on a double date. As you begin to enjoy the benefits of double dating, you may identify other couples and fill in the gaps. But that will come later. For now, just identify one couple, and like a young man in high school or college, muster your courage, walk up to them, and say, "Do you have any plans on Friday night?" It's as simple as that!

Conclusion

Congratulations! You've made it through the book. We hope you'll take some of the modest ideas presented within these pages and make them your own. This book isn't the final word on marital dating. It's only a tool to motivate you and get you thinking about how to foster intimacy and connection in your marriage through regular, intentional dating. But it won't work unless you apply your own creativity and ideas to the dating process. Use your collective imaginations, but don't overthink or overcomplicate the process. As long as you're enjoying yourselves, connecting, and developing deeper intimacy, you're on the right track. We wish you God's richest blessings as you embark on this journey together.

Notes

Chapter 1

1. W. Bradford Wilcox and Jeffrey Dew, *The Date Night Opportunity: What Does Couple Time Tell Us about the Potential Value of Date Nights?* (Charlottesville, VA: National Marriage Project/University of Virginia, 2012), 3–5.
2. Ibid., 5.
3. Ibid.
4. Ibid., 7, 9.
5. Ibid., 14.

Chapter 2

1. Dolores Curran, *Traits of a Healthy Family* (New York: Ballantine, 1984), 143.
2. John M. Gottman, *The Seven Principles for Making Marriage Work* (New York: Three Rivers Press, 1999), 79.
3. Ibid., 80.
4. Barack Obama, interview by *Ebony* magazine (2007), quoted in Kristen O'Gorman Klein, "An Inside Look at the Obamas' and the Romneys' Marriages," *Bridal Guide*, accessed April 8, 2013, http://www.bridalguide.com/blogs/bridal-buzz/obama-romney-marriages.
5. Tara Parker Pope, "For Long-Married Couples, Date Night Needs a Shakeup," *New York Times*, April 15, 2009, cited in

Tampa Bay Times, April 9, 2013, http://www.tampabay.com /news/health/research/for-long-married-couples-date-night- needs-a-shakeup/992506.

6. Lee Berk, "The Laughter-Immune Connection: New Discoveries," *Humor and Health Journal*, 5, no. 5 (1996), 1–5.

7. Dictionary.com, s.v. "intimacy," accessed April 11, 2013, http://dictionary.reference.com/browse/intimacy.

8. Focus on the Family, *Complete Guide to Baby and Child Care* (Colorado Springs: Focus on the Family/Tyndale, 2007), 287–88, adapted from FocusontheFamily.com, Q&A on "babysitter," http://family.custhelp.com/app /answers/detail/a_id/26313/kw/babysitter.

Chapter 3

1. Gary Smalley and John Trent, *The Blessing* (New York: Simon & Schuster, 1986), chapters 3–5.

2. Ibid., 29.

3. Ibid., 30.

4. Ibid., 31.

5. Ibid., 32.

6. Gary Smalley and John Trent, *The Gift of the Blessing* (Nashville: Thomas Nelson, 2004).

7. US Department of Transportation, Federal Highway Ad- ministration, *Summary of Travel Trends: 2009 National Household Travel Survey* (Washington, DC: US Department of Transportation, 2011), 30–32, 53, accessed April 9, 2013, http://nhts.ornl.gov/2009/pub/stt.pdf.

8. Sari Harrar and Rita DeMaria, *The 7 Stages of Marriage* (Pleasantville, NY: Reader's Digest Books, 2007), cited in Random Facts, "63 Interesting Facts about . . . Marriage," http://facts.randomhistory.com/interesting-facts-about-marriage.html.

9. *Merriam-Webster Online*, s.v. "cherish," accessed April 11, 2013, http://www.merriam-webster.com/dictionary/cherish.

10. Robin S. Sharma, *The Monk Who Sold His Ferrari* (San Francisco: HarperSanFrancisco, 1997), 168.

11. Lee Strobel, *Surviving a Spiritual Mismatch in Marriage* (Grand Rapids: Zondervan, 2002).

12. Dennis Rainey and Barbara Rainey, *Moments with You: Daily Connections for Couples* (Ventura, CA: Regal, 2007).

13. C. S. Lewis, *Out of the Silent Planet* (New York: Scribner, 1996), 74.

14. Christie Nicholson, "The Humor Gap: Men and Women See Laughter Differently in Romance," *Scientific American*, April 8, 2010, http://www.scientificamerican.com/article.cfm?id=the-humor-gap.

15. Ibid.

16. Study conducted by Michael Miller et al., University of Maryland School of Medicine (2005), cited in University of Maryland Medical Center, "University of Maryland School of Medicine Study Shows Laughter Helps Blood Vessels Function Better," March 7, 2005, http://www.umm.edu/news/releases/laughter2.htm.

17. R. Morgan Griffin, "Give Your Body a Boost—with Laughter," "Health and Balance," WebMD, accessed April 10, 2013, http://www.webmd.com/balance/features/give-your-body-boost-with-laughter.

18. Ibid.

19. Bureau of Labor Statistics, "American Time Use Survey," 2011, http://www.bls.gov/tus/charts/leisure.htm.

20. James H. O'Keefe et al., "Potential Adverse Cardiovascular Effects from Excessive Endurance Exercise," *Mayo Clinic Proceedings* 87, no. 6 (June 2012), doi:10.1016/j.mayocp.2012.04.005, cited in news release, *Mayo Clinic Proceedings*, June 4, 2012, http://www.mayoclinic proceedings.org/webfiles/images/journals/jmcp/jmcp_pr87_6_2.pdf.

21. WebMD, "The Effects of Stress on Your Body," July 23, 2012, accessed April 10, 2013, http://www.webmd.com/mental-health/effects-of-stress-on-your-body.

22. Study conducted by the University of Jyvaskyla, Finland, cited in "Stressed Parents Risk Having Burnt-Out Children, Study Finds," *Telegraph*, January 21, 2010, accessed April 10, 2013, http://www.telegraph.co.uk/health/healthnews/7040358/Stressed-parents-risk-having-burnt-out-children-study-finds.html.

23. Richard Swenson, *Margin: Restoring Emotional, Physical, Financial, and Time Reserves to Overloaded Lives* (Colorado Springs: NavPress, 2004), 69.

24. Studies cited in Gary Smalley and John Trent, *The Gift of the Blessing* (Nashville: Thomas Nelson, 1993), 193.

25. Gary D. Chapman, *The Five Love Languages: The Secret to Love That Lasts* (Chicago: Northfield, 2010).

26. Google search result, s.v. "friend," accessed April 10, 2013, https://www.google.com/webhp?source=search_app#hl=en&tbo=u&q=friend&tbs=dfn:1&sa=X&ei=uFgaUfirD8LNrQHv2IGwCA&sqi=2&ved=0CC8QkQ4&bav=on.2,or.r_gc.r_pw.r_qf.&bvm=bv.42261806,d.aWM&fp=3862490269f17a47&biw=1163&bih=817.

27. *Merriam-Webster Online*, s.v. "friend," accessed April 11, 2013, http://www.merriam-webster.com/dictionary/friend.

28. C. S. Lewis, "Equality," *Present Concerns: A Compelling Collection of Timely, Journalistic Essays* (Orlando, FL: Harcourt, 1986), 20.

29. Adapted from Alyson Weasley, "Twelve Steps to a Deeper Friendship with Your Spouse," "Marriage and Relationships," FocusontheFamily.com, (2007), http://www.focusonthefamily.com/marriage/sex_and_intimacy/the_role_of_friendship_in_marriage/ten_steps_to_a_deeper_friendship_with_your_spouse.aspx.

30. Adapted from Kristen Houghton, "Dreams Have No Age Limit: Famous People Who Started Late," *The Blog*, Huffpost Healthy Living, April 6, 2010, accessed April 11, 2013, http://www.huffingtonpost.com/kristen-houghton/dreams-have-no-age-limit_b_525358.html.

31. *Merriam-Webster Online*, s.v. "grace," accessed April 11, 2013, http://www.merriam-webster.com/dictionary/grace.

32. Harold L. Arnold Jr., "A Measure of Grace," "Marriage and Relationships," FocusontheFamily.com, 2008, http://www

.focusonthefamily.com/marriage/marriage_challenges /marriage_in_the_melting_pot/a_measure_of_grace .aspx.

33. Philip Yancey, *What's So Amazing about Grace?* (Grand Rapids: Zondervan, 2002).

34. Susan Mathis, "Serving Together as a Couple," "Marriage and Relationships," FocusontheFamily.com, 2011, http://www.focusonthefamily.com/marriage/daily_living /serving-together.aspx.

35. Adapted from Samantha Krieger, "Missional Marriage: 10 Practical Ways to Serve Other People," StartMarriageRight .com, December 2011, http://www.startmarriageright .com/2011/12/missional-marriage-10-practical-ways-to- serve-other-people/.

36. "Great Date Nights at Home," "Me Time," Huggies.com, accesed April 11, 2013, http://www.huggies.com/en-US /articles/baby/metime/date-night-at-home.

37. Ken R. Canfield, "What Children Gain When You Love Their Mother," Fathers.com, April 30, 2007, accessed April 11, 2013, http://www.fathers.com/content/index .php?option=com_content&task=view&id=295&Ite mid=63.

38. John Piper, *Future Grace* (Eugene, OR: Multnomah, 1995), 32.

Chapter 5

1. Greg Smalley and Erin Smalley, *Before You Plan Your Wedding . . . Plan Your Marriage* (New York: Howard, 2008).

Chapter 6

1. Adapted from Les Parrott and Leslie Parrott, *The Complete Guide to Marriage Mentoring* (Grand Rapids: Zondervan, 2005), 57–87.

2. Ibid., chapter 4.

FOCUS ON THE FAMILY®

Welcome to the Family

Whether you purchased this book, borrowed it, or received it as a gift, thanks for reading it! This is just one of many insightful, biblically based resources that Focus on the Family produces for people in all stages of life.

Focus is a global Christian ministry dedicated to helping families thrive as they celebrate and cultivate God's design for marriage and experience the adventure of parenthood. Our outreach exists to support individuals and families in the joys and challenges they face, and to equip and empower them to be the best they can be.

Through our many media outlets, we offer help and hope, promote moral values and share the life-changing message of Jesus Christ with people around the world.

Focus on the Family MAGAZINES

These faith-building, character-developing publications address the interests, issues, concerns, and challenges faced by every member of your family from preschool through the senior years.

For More INFORMATION

ONLINE:
Log on to
FocusOnTheFamily.com
In Canada, log on to
FocusOnTheFamily.ca

PHONE:
Call toll-free:
**800-A-FAMILY
(232-6459)**
In Canada, call toll-free:
800-661-9800

THRIVING FAMILY®	**FOCUS ON THE FAMILY CLUBHOUSE JR.®**	**FOCUS ON THE FAMILY CLUBHOUSE®**	**FOCUS ON THE FAMILY CITIZEN®**	
Marriage & Parenting	Ages 4 to 8	Ages 8 to 12	U.S. news issues	Rev. 3/11

More expert resources
for marriage and parenting . . .